Addresses on the

SONG OF SOLOMON

ADDRESSES

ON THE

SONG of SOLOMON

BY

H. A. IRONSIDE, Litt. D.

Author of "Notes on Hebrews," "Lectures on Romans,"
"Colossians," "Revelation," etc., etc.

LOIZEAUX BROTHERS, Inc.
Neptune, New Jersey

FIRST EDITION, JUNE 1933
NINTH PRINTING, JANUARY 1973

PUBLISHED BY LOIZEAUX BROTHERS, INC

*A Nonprofit Organization, Devoted to the Lord's Work
and to the Spread of His Truth*

PRINTED IN THE UNITED STATES OF AMERICA

PREFATORY NOTE

The little volume now before the reader consists of revised notes, considerably abbreviated, of addresses delivered in the Moody Memorial Church, Chicago, during a part of the winter of 1931-32. Many of those who listened to them professed to find blessing and edification, and there were hundreds of requests for their publication in book form, to which I have been pleased to respond. Their preparation for publication has brought added joy to my own soul while meditating afresh on this singularly delightful portion of the Word of God. The attentive reader will realize at once that there has been no attempt to fully expound the Song, but rather to stress in each address some one or more of the outstanding features of the particular portion discussed. I hope none will charge me with intentional plagiarism if they find a re-emphasis of precious truths on which others have dwelt before me. I am glad to acknowledge my indebtedness to many to whom this book has proven a well-spring of spiritual refreshment, and undoubtedly I have incorporated much that they have written, into my own addresses. I have profited particularly from the reading of "The Song of Solomon," by Adelaide Newton; "Meditations on the Song of Solomon," by Andrew Miller; "The Canticles," by J. G. Bellett; "The Song of Songs," by J. B. Jackson; "The Song of Solomon," by H. Friend, and an excellent work on the same subject by Dr. A. C. Gaebelein. All of these I can most heartily recommend to any wishing fuller exposition than I have attempted to give in these fragmentary discourses.

If God be pleased to own this attempt to create a greater yearning for fellowship with Himself and to lead the way into a deeper knowledge of the love of Christ, the labor expended will be well worth while.

H. A. IRONSIDE.

Chicago, Ill.,
Feb. 1933.

ADDRESSES

ON THE

SONG of SOLOMON

I

"We will be glad and rejoice in thee, we will remember thy love more than wine" (Song of Solomon 1:4).

THE Song of Solomon is a little book which has had a peculiar attraction for many of the people of God all through the centuries, and others of them have had great difficulty in understanding just why such a book should have a place in the canon of Holy Scripture at all. Frequently I have heard those who, it seemed to me, ought to have known better, say that as far as they were concerned they could see nothing of spiritual value in this little book, and that they questioned very much whether it were really entitled to be considered as part of the inspired

Word of God. As far as that is concerned, it is not left to the Church in our day to decide which books should belong to the canon of Scripture and which should be omitted. Our blessed Lord Jesus Christ has settled that for us, at least as far as the Old Testament is concerned. When He was here on earth He had exactly the same Old Testament that we have, consisting of the same books, no more and no less.

Those that are sometimes called the Apocryphal books did not belong to the Hebrew Old Testament which He valued and fed upon, and which He commended to His disciples, and, more than that, upon which He placed His divine imprimatur when He referred to the entire volume and said, "The Scripture cannot be broken." Therefore we do not have to raise any question as to the inspiration of the Canticles. He declared the Hebrew Bible to be the Word of the living God, and there are many figures from this little book in various parts of the New Testament; for instance, "the well of living water" (John 4); "the veiled woman" (1 Cor. 11); "the precious fruit" (Jas. 5: 7); "the spotless bride" (Eph. 5: 27); "unquenchable love" (1 Cor. 13: 8) ; "love strong as death" (John 15: 13) ; "ointment poured forth" (John 12: 3) ; "draw me" (John 6: 44) ; "the Shepherd leading His flock" (John 10: 4, 5, 27) ; and "the fruits of righteousness" (Phil. 1:11). Who can fail to see in all these allusions to the Song of Solomon?

If we grant that it is inspired, what then are its lessons? Why do we have it in Holy Scripture? Many of the Jewish teachers thought of it simply as designed of God to give a right apprehension of conjugal love. They thought of it as the glorification of the bliss of wedded life, and if we conceived of it from no higher standpoint than this, it would mean that it had a right to a place in the canon. Wedded life in Israel represented the very highest and fullest and deepest affection at a time when, in the nations surrounding Israel, woman was looked upon as a mere chattel, as a slave, or as the object of man's pleasure to be discarded when and as he pleased. But it was otherwise in Israel. The Jewish home was a place where love and tenderness reigned, and no doubt this little book had a great deal to do with lifting it to that glorious height.

But down through the centuries, the more spiritually minded in Israel saw a deeper meaning in this Song of Solomon; they recognized the design of God to set forth the mutual love subsisting between Jehovah and Israel. Again and again, in other scriptures, Jehovah is likened to a bridegroom, Israel to His chosen bride, and so the spiritual in Israel, in the years before Christ, came to look at the Song in this way. They called it "the Book of Communion." It is the book that sets forth Jehovah and His people in blessed and happy communion. And then all through the Christian centuries those who have had an insight into spiritual truth have thought of it from two standpoints. First, as typifying the wondrous relationship that subsists between Christ and the Church, the glowing heart, the enraptured spirit of our blessed Lord revealing Himself to His redeemed people as her Bridegroom and her Head, and the Church's glad response. And then, looking at it from a moral standpoint, as setting forth the relationship between an individual soul and Christ, how many a devoted saint has exclaimed with gladness, "Oh, I am my Beloved's, and His desire is toward me."

Rutherford's meditations were evidently based on this little book when he exclaimed:

> "Oh, I am my Beloved's,
>   And my Beloved's mine,
> He brings a poor vile sinner
>   Into His house of wine;
> I stand upon His merit,
>   I know no safer stand,
> Not e'en where glory dwelleth
>   In Immanuel's land."

Therefore we may think of the book from four standpoints. Looking at it literally, we see the glorification of wedded love. Looking at it from a dispensational standpoint, we see the relationship between Jehovah and Israel. Redemptively, we find the wonderful relationship between Christ and the Church. And studying it from the moral or spiritual standpoint, we see it as the book of communion between an individual soul and the blessed, glorified, risen Lord.

It is a bit difficult to get the exact connection of the different portions of the book. It is not a drama, as the book of Job is; it does not present to our consideration any continued story. It consists rather of a series of love lyrics, each one complete in itself. It is the lover with heart enraptured setting to music the thrill of the soul, and thus you have this cluster of song-flowers, each one setting forth some different phase of communion between the beloved and the one so loved. And yet, back of it all, there must be some kind of story. What is this background?

Something like a hundred years ago, Ewald, the great German critic, who has been called the father of higher criticism, suggested that the story was something like this. In the hill country north of Jerusalem there was a family in charge of a vineyard belonging to King Solomon. The young shepherdess had been won by a shepherd who had drawn her heart to himself, and their troth had been plighted. But King Solomon, as he rode along the lane one day, saw this young shepherdess in the vineyard, and his heart went out to her. He determined to win her for himself, and so tried by blandishment to stir up her affections. But she was true to her sylvan admirer. By-and-by the king actually had her kidnapped and taken to his palace, to the royal harem, and there again and again he pressed his suit and tried to alienate her from her shepherd lover in the hills. Sometimes she was almost tempted to yield, for her case seemed a hopeless one, but then she would remember him, her former lover, and she would say, "No, I cannot turn from him. 'I am my beloved's, and his desire is toward me.' " Eventually King Solomon set her free and she went back to the one she loved.

That view of things has been accepted by a great many Bible students, and I have been a little surprised at times to hear some of my fundamental brethren set it forth, apparently without realizing its source. Personally, I reject it. I do not think it at all likely that a man like Ewald, who had no real spiritual insight, ever understood this little book of communion. A man who could be called the father of higher criticism, who gave the start to the present modern trend of handling the Bible, refusing to recognize its true inspiration, does not seem to me to be such an one as the Spirit of God would use to open up this little book to us.

There are several other reasons why I refuse this view. First and foremost, it would make King Solomon "the villain of the piece," and when we turn to the Word of God, we find that

Solomon is viewed by the Holy Spirit of God as
a type of the Lord Jesus Christ. You will find
that in the Psalms Solomon is portrayed as the
prince of peace succeeding David after years
of warfare, and setting forth Christ's coming
again to reign as Prince of Peace. In the New
Testament the Lord Jesus says, "The queen of
the south shall rise up in the judgment with this
generation, and shall condemn it: for she came
from the uttermost parts of the earth to hear
the wisdom of Solomon; and behold, a greater
than Solomon is here" (Matt. 12:42). When
I say that Solomon is a type of Christ, I do not
mean Solomon personally. Whenever any man
is spoken of as a type of Christ, you are not to
think of what the man is in himself, but what
he is officially. David officially was a type of
Christ; David personally was guilty of very
grievous sin, but the Lord is the sinless One.
Solomon was guilty of very serious departure
from God during certain periods of his life, but
officially he represented our Lord Jesus Christ
as the Prince of Peace. It is not the way of
the Spirit of God to present a character, or
some other animate or inanimate object, as a
type of Christ in one place and a type of that

which is wicked and unholy in another; and if we were to take Ewald's suggestion as the real story behind this book, we would have to think of Solomon as the type of the world, the flesh, and the devil, trying to win the heart of this young woman away from the shepherd who represents the Lord Jesus Christ.

Another reason why I reject this is that it would mean that we would have to understand some of the most lovely and tender passages of this little book in which the king addresses himself to the shepherdess, as mere blandishment instead of a sincere and holy love. These very passages are those which all down through the centuries have thrilled the heart of the people of God. They have revelled in them, they have delighted in them, and fed their souls upon them. It is not likely that they have been misled, that the Holy Spirit who came to guide into all truth has thus deceived, or allowed to be deceived, so many of God's most spiritual people throughout the centuries, and therefore, I refuse to take the story that I have given you from Ewald as the explanation of the Song of Solomon.

Let me give you another story, the one that came to me one day when I was alone on my knees. I had to teach this little book and was a bit perplexed about it. I did not like the story of Ewald, and so I went to the One who wrote the book and asked Him to tell me what was behind it. "Oh," you say, "did you know the Author of the book?" Yes, I have known Him for a long time. At that time I had known Him about thirty years, now it is forty-one years. "Well," you say, "the book is rathei a recent thing if you know the author." No, not at all, it is a very old book; but the Author is the Ancient of Days and I have known Him ever since in grace He saved my soul. And so I took Him at His word and reminded Him of His promise that when the Holy Spirit came, He would take of the things of Christ and show them unto us; and I said, "Blessed Lord, I am all perplexed about this little book; by Thy Spirit show it to me so that I will really understand its meaning." I am going to give you the story that it seemed He gave to me. You may not think I am correct. Very well, you go to Him and ask Him about it, and if He tells you something different, come and tell me, and I will be glad to correct my story if you can show me that I am wrong.

This is what I thought I could see behind it all. Up there in the north country, in the mountain district of Ephraim, King Solomon had a vineyard (we are told that in the 11th verse of the last chapter), and he let it out to keepers, to an Ephraimite family. Apparently the husband and father was dead, but there was a mother and at least two brothers, two sons. We read, "My mother's children were angry with me." In Hebrew it is, "My mother's sons." There may have been more sons, but there were at least two. And then there were two daughters, two sisters, a little one spoken of in the 8th chapter — "We have a little sister." She was a little undeveloped one. And then there was the older daughter, the Shulam-ite. It would seem as though this one was the "ugly duckling," or the "Cinderella" of the family. Her brothers did not appreciate her and foisted hard tasks upon her, denying her the privileges that a growing girl might have expected in a Hebrew home. "My mother's sons were angry with me." That makes me wonder whether they were not her half-brothers, if this were not a divided family.

"My mother's sons were angry with me; they made me the keeper of the vineyards; but mine own vineyard have I not kept." They said to her, "No; you can't loll around the house; you get out and get to work. Look after the vineyard." She was responsible to prune the vines and to set the traps for the little foxes that spoiled the vines. They also committed to her care the lambs and the kids of the flock. It was her responsibility to protect and find suitable pasture for them. She worked hard, and was in the sun from early till late. "Mine own vineyard have I not kept." She meant, "While working so hard in the field, I have no opportunity to look after myself." What girl is there that does not value a few hours in front of the looking-glass, the opportunity to fix her hair and to beautify herself in any lawful way? She had no opportunity to care for her own person, and so she says, "My own vineyard have I not kept." I do not suppose she ever knew the use of cosmetics of any kind; and yet as she looked out on the road she would see the beautiful ladies of the court riding on their palfreys and in their palanquins, and as she got a glimpse of them, or as she bent over a woodland spring and saw her own reflection, she would say, "I am sunburned but comely, and if I only had the opportunity, I could be as beautiful as the rest of them." That is all involved in that expression, "Mine own vineyard have I not kept."

One day as she was caring for her flock she looked up, and to her embarrassment there stood a tall and handsome stranger-shepherd, one she had never seen before, gazing intently upon her, and she exclaimed, "Look not upon me, because I am black, because the sun hath looked upon me." And then she gives the explanation, "My mother's children were angry with me; they made me the keeper of the vineyards; but mine own vineyard have I not kept." But he answers quietly without any offensive forwardness, "I was not thinking of you as swarthy and sunburnt and unpleasant to look upon. To my mind you are altogether lovely; behold, thou art fair, my love; there is no spot in thee." Of course that went a long way toward a friendship, and so little by little that friendship ripened into affection, and affection into love, and finally this shepherd had won the

heart of the shepherdess.   Then he went away,
but before he went, he said, "Some day I am
coming for you, and I am going to make you
my bride."   And she believed him.   Probably
no one else did.   Her brothers did not believe
him, the people in the mountain country felt
she was a poor simple country maiden who had
been deceived by this strange man.   She had
inquired of him where he fed his flock, but he
put her off with an evasive answer, and yet she
trusted him.   He was gone a long time.   Sometimes she dreamed of him and would exclaim,
"The voice of my beloved," only to find that all
was quiet and dark about her.   But still she
trusted him.

One day there was a great cloud of dust on
the road and the country people ran to see what
it meant. Here came a glorious cavalcade. There
was the king's body-guard and the king himself, and they stopped just opposite the vineyard.   To the amazement of the shepherdess,
the royal outriders came to her with the an-
nouncement, "The king has sent us for you."
"For me?" she asked.   "Yes, come."   And in
obedience she went, and when she looked into
the face of the king, behold, the king was the

shepherd who had won her heart, and she said, "I am my beloved's, and his desire is toward me."

One great reason why I think this is the story of the Canticles is because all the way through this wondrous volume, from Genesis to Revelation, we have the story of the Shepherd who came from heaven's highest glory down into this dark world that He might woo and win a bride for Himself. And then He went away, but He said, "I will come again, and receive you unto Myself." And so His Church has waited long for Him to come back, but some day He is coming to fulfil His word, and,

> "When He comes, the glorious King,
> All His ransomed home to bring,
> Then anew this song we'll sing,
> 'Hallelujah, what a Saviour!'"

And so I think that is the background of the expression of loving communion in this little book, the Song of Songs. You notice that very title reminds you of the holy of holies; it is the transcendent song. The Jews did not allow a young man to read the book until he was thirty years of age, lest he might read into it mere human voluptuousness and misuse its beautiful phrases, and so we may say it is only as we grow in grace and in the knowledge of Christ that we can read this book understandingly and see in it the secret of the Lord.

I think the first chapter divides itself into three parts. The first four verses give us the soul's satisfaction; it is the expression of the bride's delight in her bridegroom. She exclaims, "The Song of songs, which is Solomon's. Let Him kiss me with the kisses of His mouth: for Thy love is better than wine." I remember a dear servant of God saying at one time, "I have sometimes wished there were only one masculine personal pronoun in the world, so that every time I say, *'Him,'* every one would know I mean the Lord Jesus Christ." You remember Mary Magdalene saying, "They have taken away my Lord, and I know not where they have laid Him." Then, looking up to the one she supposed to be the gardener, she said, "Sir, if thou have borne Him hence, tell me where thou hast laid Him, and I will take Him away." She did not think it necessary to use the name Jesus. There was only One to her, and that was the Lord who had saved her; and so the enraptured soul says, "Oh, to enjoy His

love, His communion; to enjoy the blessedness
of finding satisfaction in Himself." "Because
of the savor of Thy good ointments Thy name
is as ointment poured forth, therefore do the
virgins love Thee." We are reminded how the
house was filled with the odor of the ointment
when Mary broke her alabaster box and poured
it upon His head.

> "How sweet the name of Jesus sounds
>   In a believer's ear!
> It soothes his sorrows, heals his wounds,
>   And drives away his fear."

And now the heart cries out, "Draw me, we
will run after Thee: the King hath brought me
into His chambers: we will be glad and rejoice
in Thee, we will remember Thy love more than
wine: the upright love Thee." The shepherdess has been brought from the hill country
into the royal palace, as you and I from the
distant country into the very presence of the
Lord Himself, and how often our hearts have
sung,

> "I am Thine, O Lord, I have heard Thy voice,
>   And it told Thy love to me;
> But I long to rise in the arms of faith,
>   And be closer drawn to Thee.

"Draw me nearer, nearer, nearer, blessed Lord,
To the cross where Thou hast died;
Draw me nearer, nearer, nearer, blessed Lord,
To Thy precious bleeding side."

"We will run after thee: the king hath brought me into his chambers: we will be glad and rejoice in thee, we will remember thy love more than wine." She has been claimed by the King. What a wonderful picture we have here of real communion. No one has ever entered into the truth of communion with Christ until He Himself has become the all-absorbing passion of the soul. His love transcends every earthly joy, of which wine is the symbol in Scripture. Why is it so used? Because of its exhilarating character. Wine speaks of anything of earth which stimulates or cheers. When a worldling is cast down and depressed, he says, "Give strong drink unto him that is ready to perish, and wine unto those that be of heavy hearts. Let him drink and forget his poverty, and remember his misery no more" (Prov. 31: 6, 7). And so wine speaks of the joys of earth to which we once turned before we knew Christ. But after we know Him, we say, "We will remember Thy love more than

wine." For that reason I am always grieved
in spirit when some young Christian comes to
me with the old, old question, "Do you think
there is any harm in this or that?—any harm
in the theater, in dancing, in a game of cards,
in the social party that has no place for
Christ?" I say to myself, "If they only really
knew Him, they would never ask such questions." "We will remember Thy love more
than wine." One minute spent in fellowship
with Him is worth all the joys of earth. That
is what this book is designed to teach us.

There is a˙ fulness in His love, a sweetness
found in fellowship with Christ, of which the
worldling knows nothing. If you are in˙Christ,
these things fall off like withered autumn
leaves. I often hear people singing:

> "Oh, how I love Jesus,
> Oh, how I love Jesus,
> Oh, how I love Jesus,
>   Because He first loved me!"

And yet the same people who sing those things
sometimes never spend half-an-hour a day over
the Bible; never spend ten minutes alone with
God in prayer; have very little interest in the
coming together of the Lord's people to wait on

Him. Invite them to a prayer-meeting and
they are never there, but invite them to a social
evening and they are all present. It is evident
that the love of Christ is not yet the controlling
passion of the heart. The surrendered soul
exclaims, "We will remember Thy love more
than wine." And in Ephesians we read, "Be
not drunk with wine, wherein is excess, but be
filled with the Spirit." The Spirit-filled believer never craves the follies of the godless
world. Christ is enough to satisfy at all times.

The next section takes in verses five to eleven.
Here you have that little retrospect that I have
already given you. It looks back to the time
when she first met her lover and inquired of
him as to where he fed his flock. He answered,
"If thou know not, O thou fairest among
women, go thy way forth by the footsteps of the
flock, and feed thy kids beside the shepherds'
tents." In other words, it is as when the disciples of John came to Jesus and said, "Master,
where dwellest Thou?" And He said, "Come
and see." And so the soul cried out, "O Thou
shepherd of my heart, where feedest Thou?"
And he said to her, "Just go along in the shepherds' path, feed your flock with the rest, and

you will find out." If you take the path of devotedness to Christ, you will soon know where He dwells. If you walk in obedience to His Word you cannot fail to find Him.

In verses twelve to seventeen we have a wonderful picture of communion with the king. There he and his beautiful bride are together in the royal palace, and she says, "While the king sitteth at his table"—and the table is the place of communion—"my spikenard sendeth forth the smell thereof. A bundle of myrrh is my well-beloved unto me." In other words, "He is to me like a fragrant nosegay in which my senses delight." And so as we enter into communion with Christ, He becomes all in all to us and the heart goes out in worship and praise, like Mary, as already mentioned, in the house of Bethany bringing her alabaster box of ointment and pouring it on the head of Jesus. The king sat at the table that day, and her spikenard sent forth its fragrance and the house was filled with the odor of the ointment. That is the worshiper. There can be no real worship excepting as the heart is occupied with Him.

It is common nowadays to substitute service

for worship, and to be more taken up with hearing sermons or with ritual observances than with adoration and praise. God has said, "Whoso offereth praise glorifieth Me." He tells us He dwells amid the praises of His people. It is the satisfied heart that really worships. When the soul has been won for Christ there will be appreciation of Himself for what He is; not merely thanksgiving (important as that is) for what He has so graciously bestowed upon us. "Whom having not seen, ye love; in whom, though now ye see Him not, yet believing, ye rejoice with joy unspeakable and full of glory." This causes the spirit to go out to Him in worship and praise.

"The Father," Jesus told the Samaritan woman, "seeketh such to worship Him." He yearns for the adoring love of devoted hearts. May we indeed respond to His desire and ever "worship Him in spirit and in truth."

II

"He brought me to the banqueting house, and his banner over me was love" (Song of Solomon 2:4).

THE figure of the bride and the bridegroom is used very frequently in Scripture. Isaiah in the Old Testament says, "As the bridegroom rejoiceth over the bride, so shall thy God rejoice over thee." It is used of the Church in the New Testament, "Christ loved the Church and gave Himself for it; that He might sanctify and cleanse it with the washing of water by the Word." And when the apostle Paul speaks of the divine institution of marriage he says, "For this cause shall a man leave his father and mother, and shall be joined unto his wife, and they two shall be one flesh. This is a great mystery: but I speak concerning Christ and the Church." And then writing to the Corinthian believers, he says, "I have espoused you to one husband, that I may present you as a chaste virgin to Christ." Therefore, this delightful figure of the sweet and intimate marriage relationship is used throughout Scripture to set forth our union and communion with the Eternal Lover of our souls.

I have said that the Song of Solomon is the Book of Communion. We have that beautifully set forth in the first seven verses of this second chapter. The bride and the bridegroom are conversing together. We delight to speak with those whom we love. One of the wonderful things about love is that when some one has really filled the vision of your soul, you do not feel that any time that is taken up communing with him is wasted. Here then you have the lovers out in the country together and she exclaims, for it is evidently she who speaks in verse one, "I am the rose of Sharon, and the lily of the valleys." Generally we apply those words to the blessed Lord; we speak of Him as the Rose of Sharon. We sing sometimes, "He's the Lily of the Valley, the Bright and Morning Star." It is perfectly right and proper to apply all of these delightful figures to Him, for we cannot find any figure that speaks of that which is beautiful and of good report that cannot properly be applied to the Lord. But the wonderful thing is that He has put His own beauty upon His people. And so here the bride is looking up into the face of the bridegroom saying, "I am the rose (really, the narcissus, a blood-red flower) of Sharon, and the lily of the valleys"—the lily that thrives in the hidden place, not in the town, not in the heat and bustle of the city, but out on the cool country-side, in the quiet field. Does it not speak of the soul's separation to Christ Himself?

It is when we draw apart from the things of the world, apart to Himself, that we really thrive and grow in grace and become beautiful in His sight. I am afraid that many of us do not develop spiritually as we should, because of the fact that we know so little of this heart-separation to Himself. One of the great griefs that comes to the heart of many a one who is seeking to lead others on in the ways of Christ, is to know the influence that the world has upon them after they are converted to God. How often the question comes from dear young Christians, "Must I give up this, and must I give up that, if I am going to live a consistent Christian life?" And the things that they speak of with such apparent yearning are mere trifles after all as compared with communion with Him. Must I give up eating sawdust in order to enjoy a good dinner? Who would talk like that? Must I give up the pleasures of the world in order that I may have communion with Christ? It is easy to let them all go if the soul is enraptured with Him; and when you get to know Him better, when you learn to enjoy communion with Him, you will find yourself turning the question around; and when the world says, "Won't you participate with us in this doubtful pleasure or in this unholy thing?" your answer will be, "Must I give up so much to come down to that level? Must I give up communion with Him? Must I give up the enjoyment of His Word? Must I give up fellowship with His people in order to go in the ways of the world?" That would be the giving up. Dear young Christian, do not think of it as giving up anything to go apart with Him and enjoy His blessed fellowship. It is then the separated soul looks into His face and says, "I am like the narcissus of Sharon, and the lily of the valleys," and He at once responds, "As the lily among thorns, so is My love among the daughters." It is the heart-satisfaction that He has in His people.

See the contrast between the beautiful, fragile, lovely lily and the rough, unpleasant, disagreeable thorn. The thorn speaks of those who are still under the curse, walking in the ways of the world, and the lily sets forth His sanctified, devoted people, those who have turned from the world to Himself. This is His estimate of His saints, and as this little colloquy goes on—for it is just the soul speaking to Him and He responding, a beautiful holy dialogue —the bride looks up and says, "As the apple-tree among the trees of the wood, so is My Beloved among the sons. I sat down under His shadow with great delight, and His fruit was sweet to my taste." He says to her, "You are like a lily to Me in contrast to the thorns." And she says, "And You to me are like a beautiful fruit-tree in contrast to the fruitless trees of the wood." Scholars have wondered just what word should be used here to translate the name of this tree. Is it the apple-tree that we know, or is it the citron, a tree of a beautiful, deep green shade, producing a lovely fruit, like a cross between our grapefruit and orange, a most refreshing fruit? But the thought that the bride expresses is this: You are so much more to me than any other can possibly be. I have shade and rest and refreshment in your presence. "I sat down under His shadow with great delight, and His fruit was sweet to my taste."

How often the Spirit of God employs the figure of a shadow. To understand it aright you have to think of a hot eastern clime, the tropical sun shining down upon a wayfarer. Suddenly he sees before him a place of refuge, and exclaims as David does in the seventeenth Psalm, "Keep me as the apple of the eye, hide me under the shadow of Thy wings." Again in Psalm 36:7, "How excellent is Thy lovingkindness, O God! Therefore the children of men put their trust under the shadow of Thy wings." Isaiah speaks of "the shadow of a great rock in a weary land." The figure is used very frequently in the Bible in speaking of rest and of comfort found alone in communion with Christ.

There is no drudgery here. You married folk who are here today, do you remember when you first fell in love with the one who afterward became your life-companion? Did you find it hard to spend half-an-hour with him?

Did you try to find an excuse for staying away from that young lady? Did you always have some other engagement so that you would not be at home when that young man called on you? No; but you tried to put everything else out of the way so as to have the opportunity to became better acquainted with the person who had won your heart. So it is with the believer. The more we get to know of Christ the more we delight in His presence. So the bride says, "I sat down under His shadow with great delight, and His fruit was sweet to my taste." Her bliss was complete.

"Delight thyself also in the Lord, and He shall give thee the desires of thine heart." You cannot delight in Christ if you are going after the things of the world. "No man can serve two masters: for either he will hate the one, and love the other; or else he will hold to the one, and despise the other. Ye cannot serve God and mammon" (Matt. 6:24). And so you cannot enjoy Christ and the world at the same time.

Then we go a step farther in this scene of communion. "He brought me to the banqueting-house, and His banner over me was love."

This is the place of the soul's deep enjoyment when all else is shut out, and Christ's all-satisfying love fills the spirit's vision, and the entire being is taken up with Himself. This is indeed the "house of wine," the rest of love.

In verses five and six you have the soul so completely enthralled by the one who has won her heart that she does not care to think of anything else. Then in verse seven we have his tender answer, for it is the bridegroom speaking now: "I charge you, O ye daughters of Jerusalem, by the roes, and by the hinds of the field, that ye stir not up, nor awake my love, till she please," not "till he please." The word is in the feminine, and the point is this: He sees such joy in His people when they are in communion with Him that He says, "Now do not bring in anything to spoil this until she herself please." We have that illustrated in the Gospels. Jesus had gone to the house of Mary, Martha, and Lazarus, and Martha served and was cumbered about her serving. But Mary took her place at the feet of Jesus and listened to His words. She was in the banqueting house and His banner over her was love. He was enjoying communion with her. But Martha said, "I have

something more important for Mary than that;
it is more important that she put the dishes
on the table and get the dinner ready." But
Jesus said, as it were, "Martha, Martha, I
charge you that ye stir not up, nor awake my
love till she please." In other words, "As long
as she is content to sit at My feet and commune
with Me, this means more to Me than the most
enjoyable repast."

When the poor Samaritan woman came to
Him at the well outside the city of Sychar, His
disciples came and wondered if He were not
hungry, but He said, "I have meat to eat that
ye know not of." It meant more to Him to
have that poor sinner listening to His words,
and drawing near to Him and entering into the
love of His heart, than to enjoy the food that
they had gone to the city to get. Service is a
wonderful thing; it is a great thing to labor
for so good a Master. But oh, there is something that comes before service, something that
means more to Him and should mean more to
us, and that is fellowship with Himself!

A husband and father was bereft of his precious wife and had just a darling daughter left
to him. In those lonely days after the wife had

passed away, he found his solace and his comfort in this beautiful girl she had left behind, and evening after evening when he came home from work, they would have their quiet little meal together, and then after the dishes had been put away they would go into the sitting-room, and talk or read, and enjoy each other's company. But now it was getting on toward the holiday season, and one evening after doing up the dishes, the daughter said, "Now, Father dear, you will excuse me tonight; I have something to occupy me upstairs. You can read while I go up." So he sat alone, and the next night the same thing happened, and night after night for about two weeks he sat alone each evening. On Christmas morning the girl came bounding into his room saying, "Merry Christmas, Father dear," and handed him a beautiful pair of slippers she had made for him. He looked at them, and then kissed her and said, "My darling, you made these yourself?" "Yes, Father." "Is this why I have been denied your company the last two weeks?" he asked. "Yes," she said; "this is my secret." Then he said, "That is very lovely, but next time I would rather have you than anything you can make

for me." Our blessed Lord wants ourselves.
Our heart's affection means far more to Him
than service. And yet there will be service,
of course, but service that springs out of communion, and that accomplishes a great deal
more than when we are too busy to enjoy fellowship with Him.

Another section of the chapter is from verse
eight to thirteen, and that we may call "Love's
Expectation." In this section he is absent from
her and she is waiting for him to return. Suddenly she thinks she hears his voice, and she
springs up saying, "The voice of my beloved!
Behold, he cometh leaping upon the mountains,
skipping upon the hills." You and I who know
His grace realize something of what this means.
He has saved us, won our hearts, as this shepherd lover won the heart of this shepherdess,
and He has gone away, but He said, "I will
come again, and receive you unto Myself," and
when He comes, He will be the glorious King.
It was the shepherd who won her heart; it was
the King to whom she was wedded. And so
Jesus, the Good Shepherd, has won us for Himself, but He will be the King when we sit with
Him upon the throne.

Does it not stir your soul to think that at any moment we may hear His voice saying, "Arise, My love, and come away?" Listen to the way she depicts it here. "My beloved spake and said unto me, Rise up, my love, my fair one, and come away. For, lo, the winter is past, the rain is over and gone; the flowers appear on the earth; the time of the singing is come and the voice of the turtle [dove] is heard in our land; the fig tree putteth forth her green figs, and the vines with the tender grape give a good smell. Arise, my love, my fair one, and come away." It is not merely the singing of birds, as you have it in the Authorized Version, but "the time of singing," when He will sing and we shall sing, and we shall rejoice together, when earth's long winter of sorrow and trial and perplexity is ended and the glorious spring will come with our blessed Lord's return. You see this is just a little poem in itself, a complete love-lyric in anticipation of the bridegroom's return. How soon all this may be fulfilled for us, how soon He may come for whom our hearts are yearning, we do not know. We have waited for Him through the years; we have known the cold winters, the

hard and difficult days; we have known the trying times, but oh, the joy, the gladness when
He comes back! He has said, "A little while
and He that shall come will come and will not
tarry."

> " 'A little while'—the Lord shall come,
>   And we shall wander here no more;
> He'll take us to His Father's home,
>   Where He for us is gone before—
> To dwell with Him, to see His face,
> And sing the glories of His grace."

We shall then share the glory that He went
to prepare. What will that mean for us and
for Him! He will have the joy of His heart
when He has us with Him.

The closing verses speak of that which should
be going on during all the time of His absence.
In the first place, we ought to be enjoying Him
anticipatively, and then there should be self-
judgment, putting out of the life anything that
would grieve or dishonor Him. The bridegroom speaks; may He speak to our souls. 'O
My dove, that art in the clefts of the rock."
That is where we are resting, in the cleft of
the rock.

> "Rock of Ages, cleft for me,
>   Grace hath hid me safe in Thee."

"O My dove, that art in the clefts of the rock, in the secret places of the stairs," or, "in the hidden places of the going up." We are moving upward from day to day, soon to be with Himself. "Let Me see thy countenance, let Me hear thy voice; for sweet is thy voice, and thy countenance is comely." Have you heard Him saying that to you, and have you sometimes turned coldly away?

Probably when you arose in the morning you heard Him say, "Let Me see thy countenance before you begin the work of the day; spend a little time with Me, let Me hear thy voice; talk with Me before you go out to speak to other people; let Me enjoy a little time with you, the one for whom I died, before you take up the affairs of the day." And you have just turned coldly away, looked at your watch, and said, "I am sorry, but I cannot spare any time this morning; I must hasten to the office or the shop," and so all day He waited for you. When evening came, He spoke again and said, "Let Me see thy countenance, let Me hear thy voice," and you said, "Oh, I am so tired and weary to-night, I have to hurry off to bed." Have there not been many days like that? Are there going to be many more? Or will you seek by grace to respond to the love of His heart and let Him see your face and hear your voice a little oftener?

Then we have her response, "Take us the foxes, the little foxes, that spoil the vines: for our vines have tender grapes." You see, her brothers had driven her out to be the vine-dresser. Now she thinks of that, and sees a figure there, and says, "I know how I had to watch the vines so carefully, and now I have to watch the growth of my own spiritual life. As I set traps for the little foxes, so now I have to judge in myself anything that would hinder fellowship with Him, that would hinder my spiritual growth." What are the little foxes that spoil the vine? I can tell you a good many. There are the little foxes of vanity, of pride, of envy, of evil speaking, of impurity (I think this though is a wolf instead of a little fox). Then there are the little foxes of carelessness, of neglect of the Bible, of neglect of prayer, of neglect of fellowship with the people of God. These are the things that spoil the vine, that hinder spiritual growth. Deal with them in the light of the cross of Christ; put them to death before they

ruin your Christian experience, do not give
them any place. "Take us the foxes, the little
foxes, that spoil the vines."

And now we have the closing words, "My
beloved is mine, and I am his: he feedeth
among the lilies." We need to be reminded of
this again and again. The most intimate,
sweet, and unsullied spiritual relationship is
brought before us here. And this is to con-
tinue, "Until the day break, and the shadows
flee away." When will that be? When our
blessed Lord returns. "Turn, my beloved, and
be thou like a roe or a young hart upon the
mountains of Bether," that is, the mountains
of separation. He is the object of her soul as
she abides upon the mountains of separation
until he comes back.

Oh, that these things were more real with us
all! We profess to "hold" the truth of our
Lord's near return. But does it hold us in such
a way that we esteem all earthly things but
loss for Him who is so soon to claim us wholly
for Himself? "Let us search and try our ways,"
and make sure that we allow nothing in our
lives that destroys the power of this "blessed
hope" over our souls.

"I sought him whom my soul loveth; I sought him, but I found him not" (Song of Solomon 3:1).

THE third chapter of this exquisite book is divided into two parts; the first comprises verses 1 to 5, and the second, the balance of the chapter, verses 6 to 11. The opening section which we now consider sets before us communion interrupted and renewed.

We are not told just what it was that had disturbed the fellowship of the lovers. It may have been the absence of the Beloved, resulting in a temporary lethargic condition on the part of his espoused one. Possibly the entire section is to be treated as a dream. In fact, this seems the most likely explanation. But dreams often reflect the disturbed state of the heart. "A dream cometh through the multitude of business" (Eccles. 5:3).

The opening verse depicts the restlessness of

one who has lost the sense of the Lord's presence. What saint has not known such experiences? David once exclaimed, "Lord, by
Thy favor Thou hast made my mountain to
stand strong; Thou didst hide Thy face, and I
was troubled" (Ps. 30: 7). This withdrawal
of the light of His countenance is not neces-
sarily in anger. Sometimes it is admonitory.
It is love's way of bringing the soul to a real-
ization of something cherished or allowed that
grieves the Holy Spirit of God. Or it may be
the testing of faith to see whether one can
trust in the dark as well as in the light.
Rutherford's experience is depicted thus:

> "But flowers need night's cool sweetness,
>   The moonlight and the dew;
> So Christ from one who loved Him,
>   His presence oft withdrew."

To His disciples He said, when He announced
His going away, "Ye believe in God, believe
also in Me." That is to say, "As you have believed in God whom you have never seen, so
when I am absent believe in Me. I will be just
as real—and just as true—although to sight
unseen." For though the soul lose the sense
of His presence nevertheless He still abideth

faithful. He never forsakes His people though He seems to have withdrawn and He does not manifest Himself. This is indeed a test of faith and of true-hearted devotion. We say, "Absence makes the heart grow fonder," but there is often greater truth in the old proverb, "Out of sight, out of mind." When the Lord as a boy stayed in the temple, even Mary and Joseph went on "supposing Him to be in the company," not realizing the true state of affairs.

Here the bride feels her loss. She seeks for him; he is not there. There is no response to her cry. For her, rest is impossible with this awful sense of loneliness upon her. She must seek until she finds; she cannot be contented without him. Would that this were always true of us! But, alas, how often we go on bereaved of the assurance of His presence, yet so insensate that we scarcely realize our loss. Here there is energy—determination—action! She *must* find him who is all in all to her. Love abhors a vacuum. Only the sense of his presence can fill and satisfy her heart.

In her dream—or possibly in reality—she leaves her mountain home and goes forth in

search of the object of her deep affections. To
the city she wends her way, and wanders about
its streets and peers into every hidden place,
looking only for him! But at first her search
is unrewarded. In fact it is not until she bears
witness to others of his preciousness that he
gladdens her vision. Note the terms used:
"I sought him; I found him not; I will seek
him; I found him not."

The watchmen, guarding the city at night,
are surprised to see a lovely and yet apparently
respectable woman going about at such an
hour. But she turns eagerly to them ere they
can reprove her, crying in the distress of her
soul, "Saw ye him whom my soul loveth?" The
abrupt question conveyed little information indeed. To the prosaic guardians of the peace,
it must have sounded almost incoherent. But
to her it was all that was necessary. There
was only one for whom her soul yearned.
Surely they too would know his worth! But,
from them, she gets no response.

Leaving them, she has scarcely gone from
their sight ere she comes upon the object of her
search. In an ecstasy of rapture she lays hold
of him, and clinging to him as to one who

might again vanish away, she brings him into her own home where she first saw the light of day.

The more the passage is pondered, the more evident it seems to be that all this happened in a dream. But it tells of the deep exercises of her soul. She misses him; she cannot be happy without the sense of his presence. Her only joy is found in abiding in his love. She finds him when she seeks for him with all her heart.

This is what gratifies him. And so again we have the refrain of satisfied love. "I charge you, O ye daughters of Jerusalem, by the roes and by the hinds of the field, that ye stir not up nor wake my love until she please" (ver. 5), for, as previously mentioned, the expression here is in the feminine in the original. Nothing gives our Lord more delight than to find a heart that joys in Him for what He is in Himself. Too often we think rather of His gifts, the gracious favors He bestows. It is right and proper that these should stir us to thanksgiving; but it is as we get to know Himself and to joy in His love that we really worship in blissful communion.

"The bride eyes not her garments,
    But her dear Bridegroom's face;
I will not gaze at glory,
    But on my King of Grace!
Not at the crown He giveth,
    But on His pierced Hand;
The Lamb is all the glory
    Of Immanuel's land."

The latter part of the chapter is of an entirely different character, and sets forth the truth of union rather than of restored communion. It is a little gem, complete in itself. The espoused one has waited long for the return of the shepherd whose love she has prized above all else. His promise to return for her has been cherished and relied upon, even though at times his continued absence has made the heart sick with yearning and even overwhelmed the drooping spirit with fear. But never has she really lost confidence in his plighted word. Eagerly she has awaited the fulfilment of his promise.

One day all the simple folk of the countryside are astir and filled with interest and wonder as they behold a grand procession wending its way along the highway up from the glorious city of God. Outriders and trumpeters on prancing chargers herald the approach of a royal equipage. "Who is this that cometh?" This is the question raised by every on-looker. Whose progress is this? Who travels in such grandeur and splendor? One can imagine the scene, and none can blame the curious conjectures as the peasants of the hills gaze with wonder upon the advancing cavalcade. In the Hebrew the question is really, "Who is she that cometh?" It is a bridal procession. But who is the honored maiden called to share the love of the King? Evidently at first they look in vain for a sight of her. Everything proclaims a nuptial parade, but no bride is really seen.

The bridegroom, however, is clearly in evidence. It is the son of David himself. In excited admiration the wondering people exclaim: "Behold his palanquin, which is Solomon's!" The royal conveyance is recognized. Sixty valiant soldiers guard their king as he journeys through the country. Clad in armor, each with his sword ready to defend his sovereign against any lurking traitorous foes, they move on in orderly array, as the excitement among the shepherds and vinedressers grows

ever more intense. Not often have their eyes
been regaled by such a scene as this! Perhaps
they will never see its like again!

How magnificent, how costly is that royal
palanquin! It is the King's provision for the
comfort of his bride. And that bride is half-
hidden among the rest of the country-folk, not
daring to believe that such honor is for her.
All eyes are on the King. It is his crowning
day—his nuptial hour—the day of the gladness
of his heart. He has come forth to seek and
claim his spouse whom he won as the shepherd,
and to whom he now reveals himself as the
King.

There is no actual mention of the claiming
of the bride and bringing her to the King, it is
true. But it is clearly implied. He has come
to fulfil his promise to make her his own. With
deep and chastened joy she responds to the
royal summons and takes her place at his side,
and so the procession sweeps on, leaving the
bewildered on-lookers gasping with startled
amazement at the sudden change in the estate
of her who had been through the years but
one of themselves. It is a worthy theme for
a Song of Songs! And most graphically it

portrays the glorious reality which the Bride
of the Lamb shall soon know when the Shep-
herd-King comes to claim His own.

> "He is coming as the Bridegroom,
>   Coming to unfold at last
> The great secret of His purpose,
>   Mystery of ages past;
> And the bride, to her is granted,
>   In His beauty now to shine,
> As in rapture she exclaimeth,
>   'I am His, and He is mine!'
> Oh, what joy that marriage union,
>   Mystery of love divine;
> Sweet to sing in all its fulness,
>   'I am His, and He is mine!'"

How short then will seem the waiting-time;
how trifling the follies of earth which we gave
up in order to be pleasing in His sight! How
slight too will the sufferings of the present time
appear, as compared with the glory then to be
enjoyed.

If some fancy we have drawn too much
upon imagination as we have sought to picture
the real background of these lovely lyrics, let
me ask, Is it possible to mistake the picture
when all Scripture tells the same story? What
was the marriage of Adam and Eve intended
to signify? What shall be said of the servant

seeking a bride for Isaac, and what of the love
of Jacob as he served so unweariedly for
Rachel? Of what "great mystery" does Asen-
ath, the Gentile wife of Joseph, speak? And
what shall be said of the love of Boaz for Ruth?
Hosea who bought his bride in the slave-market
gives a darker side of the picture, yet all is in
wonderful harmony. All alike tell the story
that "Christ loved the Church and gave Himself for it, that He might sanctify and cleanse
it by the washing of water by the Word, and
present it unto Himself a glorious Church, not
having spot, or wrinkle, or any such thing"
(Eph. 5 : 26, 27). "All fair" indeed will she
then be in His eyes, and one with Him forever, for, "It is written, For this cause shall a
man leave his father and his mother and shall
be joined to his wife, and they twain shall be
one flesh. This is a great mystery, but I speak
concerning Christ and the Church" (Eph. 5 :
31, 32).

Surely all this should speak loudly to our
hearts, we who through grace have been won
for One we have never yet seen, but of whom
we read, "Whom having not seen, ye love; in
whom, though now ye see Him not, yet believ-

ing, ye rejoice with joy unspeakable and full of glory." What will it be when we behold Him coming in royal array to claim us as His very own, when we discern in the King of kings, the Good Shepherd who gave His life for the sheep, and who, ere He left this scene, gave the solemn promise, "If I go...I will come again and receive you unto Myself." That glad nuptial hour draws on apace. Well may our hearts be stirred and our spiritual pulses quickened as we join the wondering cry, "Who is this that cometh?"

When the bride is caught away, what will the astonishment be on the part of those who had never understood that she was the loved one of the Lord Most High? When they realize that the Church is gone and the heavenly procession has passed them by, what will be their thoughts in that day?

But we must pause here for the present. The next chapter gives us the glad recognition and the happy response.

"Thou art all fair, my love; there is no spot in thee" (Song of Solomon 4: 7).

IT is not strange that as we think of our Lord Jesus Christ, the Heavenly Bridegroom, our souls are moved to their deepest depths, but it is hard for us to realize that He has a greater love for us than we could ever possibly have for Him. And so here in this fourth chapter of the Song of Solomon, we hear the bridegroom expressing to his loved one the feelings of his heart toward her, and as we read these words, as we listen to these heart-breathings, we should remember that the speaker is really our Lord Jesus Christ, and that the bride may be looked at in various ways, as we have already seen. Prophetically, we may think of the bride as Israel, and Jehovah rejoicing over her in that coming day; individually, we may think of the bride as representing any saved soul, and the Lord expressing

His delight in the one He has redeemed to Himself by His precious blood; or as that Church which Christ loved and for which He gave Himself.

So we may see in these utterances His delight in His Church. In verses one to seven of this fourth chapter, you will notice that He addresses Himself directly to the bride, and He speaks of her beauties as He sees them in a very wonderful way. The imagery, of course, as throughout this book, is strictly oriental, and goes considerably beyond what we prosaic occidentals are in the habit of using. And yet as we read it, we see that there is nothing coarse, nothing that would bring the blush to the cheek of modesty. It is the fullest, most rapturous delight of the bridegroom in the bride, but every expression is in keeping with the holiness of this blessed little book.

First, he speaks of her general appearance. Four times over in this chapter, he tells her of her fairness. Twice he declares it in verse one. He says, "Behold, thou art fair, my love; behold, thou art fair." In verse seven we read, "Thou art all fair, my love; there is no spot in thee." Again in verse ten, "How fair is thy love, my sister, my spouse! How much better is thy love than wine!" And yet she had no fairness in herself, as we had no beauty in ourselves. In an earlier chapter we heard her say, "I am black as the tents of Kedar, as the curtains of Solomon." But he says, as he looks at her through love's eyes, "Thou art all fair." Does it not bring before us the wondrous thing that our Saviour has done for every one of us who have been redeemed by the precious blood of Christ? We would never have been saved at all if we had not realized in some measure our own wretchedness, our own sinfulness, our unlovely character. It was because of this that we fled to Him for refuge and confessed that we were anything but fair, anything but beautiful. We took our places side by side with Job and cried, "I have heard of Thee by the hearing of the ear: but now mine eye seeth Thee. Wherefore I abhor myself, and repent in dust and ashes" (Job 42: 5, 6). We knelt beside Isaiah and exclaimed, "I am a man of unclean lips, and I dwell in the midst of a people of unclean lips" (Isa. 6: 5). We took part with Peter and cried, "Depart from me; for I am a sinful man, O Lord" (Luke 5: 8). But when

we took that place of repentance, of acknowl-
edgement of our own natural deformity and
unloveliness, He looked upon us in His grace
and said, "Thou art perfect in Mine eyes by the
comeliness which I have put upon thee." And
now as those who have been washed from our
sins in His own precious blood, He addresses
us in the rapturous way that we have here,
"Thou art all fair, My love; there is no spot in
thee." What! No spot in us, when we were
stained by sin, when we were polluted by iniquity? Once it could be said of us, "From the
sole of the foot even unto the head there is no
soundness in it; but wounds, and bruises, and
putrifying sores: they have not been closed,
neither bound up, neither mollified with ointment" (Isa. 1: 6). And now His holy eyes cannot find one spot of sin, nor any sign of iniquity. Let this give us to understand what
grace hath wrought.

> "Amazing grace, how sweet the sound,
> That saved a wretch like me!"

It is only God's matchless grace that has thus
made us accepted in the Beloved.

Then you will notice that the bridegroom

looking upon his bride speaks of her person in the most glowing terms, referring to seven different things. First, he speaks of her eyes and says to her, "Thou hast doves' eyes within thy locks." What does that mean? The dove was a clean bird, the bird of love and sorrow, the bird offered in sacrifice upon the altar, and thus typified our Lord Jesus as the heavenly One. And now he sees reflected in his bride that which speaks of himself. "Thou hast doves' eyes." We may not have stopped to realize it, but the dove is very keen of sight.

Recently in an eastern city, a poor carrier pigeon fell exhausted on one of those high buildings, and somebody working on the roof of the building caught it utterly unable to rise. They found attached to it a message that had come over three thousand miles, and that little dove had seen its way all along the miles, and had flown on and on until at last it had brought the message to that eastern city. When our blessed Lord says to us, "Thou art fair, My love; behold, thou art fair; thou hast doves' eyes within thy locks," it means not only that we have eyes of beauty, but eyes quick to discern the precious and wonderful things that are hidden for us in His holy Word. Do we respond to this, or do these doves' eyes sometimes take to wandering, going out after the things of a poor godless world?

He says, "Thy hair is as a flock of goats, that appear from Mount Gilead." He refers to the Syrian goat with its long silken hair. One can imagine the beauty of the scene, a flock of goats up yonder on the mountain-side. The bridegroom says, "Your hair reminds me of that." Hair, in Scripture, is a woman's glory. That is one reason why she is not supposed to follow the styles of the world and cut away her beauty and glory. You remember the woman of old who loved Jesus and knelt at His feet and washed them with her tears and wiped them with her hair. She was using that which spoke of her beauty and her glory to minister to Him, the loving, blessed Saviour. Some of my sisters will forgive me if I say that it would be difficult for them to dry anyone's feet with their hair! Yes, her hair is a woman's glory and beauty, and, incidentally, that is exactly the reason why the Word of God tells the woman to cover her head when she comes into the presence of the Lord. When she comes in before Him whose glory fills the heavens, to join with His worshipping people, she is to cover her own glory that no one's attention may be distracted, but fixed on Christ Himself. When you get the inwardness of these things, you find there is a beauty and a privilege in them that does away with all legality, and also does away with leaving us free to follow our own judgment. In Scripture, some things are commanded because they are right, and other things are right because they are commanded. When He makes known His will, the subject Christian bows to His Word, assured that there is a reason for it, though he does not always understand it. How He delights to behold His obedient people; how He glories in their moral beauty!

Then, in the third place, he speaks of her teeth, and we may think that strange, but there is nothing more beautiful than a lovely set of pearls half-hidden in the mouth. "Thy teeth are like a flock of sheep that are shorn, which came up from the washing; whereof every one bear twins, and none is barren among them." The two sets of teeth answer to the twins in their cleanliness and sparkling beauty, so attractive in his eyes. And how important the teeth are, spiritually speaking, because they speak to us of mastication, of the ability to properly lay hold of and digest our food. I am afraid there are a number of toothless Christians from that standpoint. Some say, "I do not know how it is, but other people read their Bibles and find such wonderful things, when I do not find much in mine." The trouble is you have such poor teeth, you do not masticate your spiritual food properly. It is by meditation that we appropriate our daily provision. David said, "My meditation of Him shall be sweet" (Ps. 104: 34). Until He gives you a new set of spiritual teeth, you had better use some second-hand ones. Thank God for what others have found; read their books, and get something that way! By-and-by if you will wait on Him, the Lord will give you back your teeth, even if you have lost them, and you will be able to enjoy the truth for yourself.

The third verse is most lovely: "Thy lips are like a thread of scarlet, and thy speech is comely." This is different from that abominable custom of today that leads so many women, of course not consistent Christian

women, but those of the world and Christians living on the edge of the world, to put
that filthy stuff upon their lips that makes
them look like a cross between poor, low
women of the street and circus performers.
Here it is the red lip of health, of spiritual
health. "Thy lips are like a thread of scarlet,
and thy speech is comely." Why? Because it
is speech that has to do with Him! The bride
loves to speak of the bridegroom, as the Christian loves to speak of Christ, and her lips are
like a thread of scarlet, for she exalts that
blood by which she has been brought nigh to
God. Every real Christian will have lips like
a thread of scarlet, for he gladly confesses that
he owes everything for eternity to that precious atoning blood of the Lord Jesus Christ.
It is not only when we gather at the table of
the Lord, when we bow in worship as we take
the bread and cup as from His blessed pierced
hand, that we love to sing and speak and think
of the blood; but always, everywhere, at all
times, the believer delights to remember that
he has been redeemed to God by the precious
blood of Christ. You will find the scarlet
thread running right through this Book.

God has said, "The life of the flesh is in the blood, and I have given it to you upon the altar to make an atonement for your soul; it is the blood that maketh an atonement for the soul." "When I see the blood, I will pass over you." "We have been redeemed to God by the precious blood of Christ, as of an unblemished spotless lamb, foreknown indeed from the foundation of the world, but manifest in these last times for you." "The blood of Jesus Christ, God's Son, cleanseth us from all sin." And when at last we get home to heaven, our lips will be like a thread of scarlet still, for we will join in that new song and sing our praises to Him who was "slain and has loosed us from our sins in His own blood," and we will render adoration unto the Lamb whose blood was shed, that we might be made kings and priests unto God. O Christian, make much of the blood, speak often of the blood. Do not be satisfied with the namby-pamby, bloodless religion of the day. When you ask the question, "Are you a Christian?" and you get the ready answer, "Oh, yes; I belong to the church," then see that your lips are like a thread of scarlet and ask, "Are you trusting in the precious blood of the Lord Jesus alone for salvation?" So often you will find that the idle profession made a moment ago was only an empty thing. They are Christians in name only. There are thousands about us who know nothing of the cleansing value of the blood of Jesus.

"Thy temples are like a piece of a pomegranate within thy locks." You know the temple speaks of the dome of thought, and so the bride's thought is about her bridegroom. She loves to think of him, to meditate upon the treasures found in his word. Then he delights in her as she delights in him.

In the next verse we have the strength of her character, given her by divine grace. "Thy neck is like the tower of David builded for an armory, whereon there hang a thousand bucklers, all shields of mighty men." David's tower, you see, is the place of defense, the place of strength, and the bride here is one of those who can stand up straight and boldly look the world in the face, assured of the love and protection of her matchless bridegroom. And so we are called upon to be "strong in the Lord, and in the power of His might." The head won't be hanging down like a bulrush when our hearts

are taken up with Him.   There will be a bold-
ness that is never known when out of communion with Him.

Then, last of all, in the seventh place he
speaks of that which tells of affection. "Thy
two breasts are like two young roes that are
twins, which feed among the lilies." Her heart
is his, her whole being belongs to him, and he
rejoices in her. We may well sing:

> "Jesus, Thou art enough
>   The mind and heart to fill;
> Thy patient life—to calm the soul;
>   Thy love—its fear dispel.
>
> "O fix our earnest gaze
>   So wholly, Lord, on Thee;
> That, with Thy beauty occupied,
>   We elsewhere none may see."

As we joy in Him, we will find that He will
joy in us. You remember what Faber wrote:

> "That Thou should'st so delight in me
>   And be the God Thou art,
> Is darkness to my intellect,
>   But sunlight to my heart."

I cannot understand why He should say,
"Thou art all fair, My love; there is no spot
in thee." I cannot comprehend such matchless

grace, but my heart can rejoice in it, and so I love Him in return because He first loved me.

Following this section in which we have the bridegroom's joy in the bride, in verses eight to eleven we have his summons to companionship with himself. The bridegroom would call his bride away from everything else that has occupied her in order to find in him her all in all. "Come with me from Lebanon, my spouse, with me from Lebanon: look from the top of Amana, from the top of Shenir and Hermon, from the lions' dens, from the mountains of the leopards. Thou hast ravished my heart, my sister, my spouse; thou hast ravished my heart with one of thine eyes, with one chain of thy neck. How fair is thy love, my sister, my spouse! how much better is thy love than wine! and the smell of thine ointments than all spices!" He sees her upon the mountain-side. And, you know, the mountain is the place of privilege, the place of beauty, of worldly grandeur and glory, but it is also the place of danger. The leopard's lair is there and the lion's den, and as he beholds her there alone, he cries, "Come with me from Lebanon...from the lions' dens,

from the mountains of the leopards." Our
blessed Lord wants the companionship of His
redeemed people. How sweet those words,
"Come with Me!" He never calls His people
from anything, either the beautiful things of
the world or the dangerous things (and after
all, the beautiful is often the most dangerous),
simply to take a path alone, but it is always,
"Come with Me," and you cannot afford, you
who love His name, to draw back, to say,
"There are other things so lovely, so beautiful,
that my soul must have; I cannot leave them
to go with Thee." He who died for you, He
who left heaven's glory in order to redeem your
soul, calls to you and says, "Come with Me."
Can you draw back and say, "No; it is too
much to ask; I cannot leave these surround-
ings; I cannot leave these worldly follies; I
cannot quit this place of danger for Thy sake,
Lord Jesus?" Surely there is not very much
love there. You need to get down before Him
and confess the sin of your cold-heartedness
and indifference, and ask for a fresh vision
of the love that He manifested in the cross
that your heart may be weaned away from
everything else. Dr. Watts has put it:

"He calls me from the lion's den,
From this wild world of beasts and men,
To Zion where His glories are,
No Lebanon is half so fair.
Nor dens of prey, nor flowery plains,
Nor earthly joys, nor earthly pains,
Shall hold my feet or force my stay,
When Christ invites my soul away."

Does your heart respond to that? What He desires above everything else is to see His people finding satisfaction in His company.

And then in the closing two verses of this section, verses ten and eleven, we read, "How fair is thy love, my sister, my spouse! how much better is thy love than wine! and the smell of thine ointments than all spices! Thy lips, O my spouse, drop as the honeycomb; honey and milk are under thy tongue; and the smell of thy garments is like the smell of Lebanon." You remember in the first chapter it is she who said, looking up to him, "We will remember thy love more than wine." Now it is he who responds to her and says, "How much better is thy love than wine! and the smell of thine ointments than all spices! Thy lips, O my spouse, drop as the honeycomb: honey and milk are under thy tongue; and the smell of thy garments is like the smell of Lebanon." His people should be fragrant with the sweetness of Christ. It is said of the disciples of old, "They took knowledge that they had been with Jesus," and if we are in His company, there will be a rich fragrance of holiness, of heavenliness, about us wherever we are found.

A minister tells of riding with another preacher on top of a bus in London, England. As they came down a poor-looking street with a big factory on one side, they were halted, and they noticed the doors of the factory had opened and hundreds of girls were pouring out and making their way across the street to a lunch room; suddenly the air was filled with a sweet delightful fragrance. The visitor said, "Isn't that remarkable in a factory district here in London?—such wondrous fragrance! It seems like the odor of a great garden. You would not think of finding such fragrance in this district." "Oh, you don't understand," said his friend; "this is one of the largest perfume-factories in all the British Isles, and these young people are working constantly among the perfumes, and everywhere they go the fragrance remains upon their garments."

Beloved, if you and I are living in fellowship with Christ, if we keep in touch with Him, everywhere we go His fragrance will be manifested in our lives.

V

"A garden inclosed is my sister, my spouse; a spring shut up, a fountain sealed. Thy plants are an orchard of pomegranates, with pleasant fruits; camphire, with spikenard, spikenard and saffron; calamus and cinnamon, with all trees of frankincense; myrrh, and aloes, with all the chief spices: a fountain of gardens, a well of living waters, and streams from Lebanon. Awake, O north wind; and come, thou south; blow upon my garden, that the spices thereof may flow out. Let my beloved come into his garden, and eat his pleasant fruits. I am come into my garden, my sister, my spouse: I have gathered my myrrh with my spice; I have eaten my honeycomb with my honey; I have drunk my wine with my milk: eat, O friends; drink, yea, drink abundantly, O beloved" (Song of Solomon 4:12-15; 5:1).

WE have been noticing in chapter after chapter how the blessed Lord puts before us our privileges as those who are permitted to enter into communion with Himself, and now in this little section we have the believer (if you think of it as the individual), or Israel, or the Church, whichever you will, pictured as a watered garden set apart for our Lord Himself to bring forth fruit that will be to His delight. It is a lovely figure, one used on a number of other occasions in Scripture. In the fifty-eighth chapter of the prophet Isaiah, God pictures His people as such a garden. In verse eleven, He says, "The Lord shall guide thee continually, and satisfy thy soul in drought, and make fat thy bones: and thou shalt be like a watered garden, and like a spring of water, whose waters fail not." This is a beautiful picture. Primarily it refers to Israel, and morally it speaks of any believer, of that which God would see in all His saints as they walk with Him. In the book of the prophet Jeremiah, chapter thirty-one, verse twelve, we read, "Therefore they shall come and sing in the height of Zion, and shall flow together to the goodness of the Lord, for wheat, and for wine, and for oil, and for the young of the flock and of the herd: and their soul shall be as a watered garden; and they shall not sorrow any more at all." It is the Risen Christ Himself from whom we draw abundant supplies of mercy and grace; but did you ever think of your own heart as a garden in which He is to find His joy? Your very life is as a garden which is

to be for His pleasure. That is the figure you
have here. It is the bridegroom looking upon
his bride with his heart filled with delight as
he says to her, "You are to be for me, you
are like a lovely garden yielding its fruit and
flowers for me, set apart for myself."

"A garden inclosed is my sister, my spouse;
a spring shut up, a fountain sealed." We in
America like open gardens that anybody can
enjoy, but in Syria and in other parts of the
old land, they have many inclosed gardens,
gardens that are walled in. This is necessary
in some of those countries, as otherwise they
would be destroyed by marauding creatures
and robbers. It is as though the Lord says,
"That is what I want My people to be, separated to Myself; I want them to have about
them the wall of holiness, for I have marked
them off as My own." In the Psalms we read,
"The Lord hath set apart him that is godly for
Himself." Some Christians shrink from the
idea of separation. If it is only a legal thing,
it may become mere Pharisaism with no heart
to it, but if it is to Himself, if it is the soul
going out to Him, if one turns away from the
world for love of Him, then separation is a

very precious thing indeed, and one does not need to think of it as legal bondage, for it is being set apart for God Himself. Could one think of a higher privilege on earth than that He might find His joy in us and we might find our joy in Him?

"A garden inclosed is my sister, my spouse." How Satan likes to break down the wall, to destroy that principle of holy separation which would keep our hearts for the Lord alone; but what a loss it is to our own souls, and what a loss it means to Him, when His people become like a garden trodden under foot, as it were, by every wayfarer. That is what the Christian becomes who does not keep the path of separation.

Then notice the next figure, "A spring shut up, a fountain sealed." Pure water is a very precious thing in the far East and so often, when a spring is discovered, it is walled about, covered, and locked, and the owner of it keeps the key so that he can go and drink when he will, and the water is kept from pollution and waste. That is what our Lord would have in His people. He has given His Holy Spirit to dwell in us, and the Holy Spirit is Himself the

Fountain of Water within every believer's heart, that we might be to His praise and to His glory. This living water within the garden will, of course, result in abundant fruit and flowers.

"Thy plants are an orchard of pomegranates, with pleasant fruits; camphire, with spikenard." The orchard suggests more than a mere garden of beautiful flowers; not only something fair to look at, or something that is fragrant to the senses, but something fruitful as well. What precious fruit is borne by the believer; what precious fruit is found in the heart of the one who is shut up to God! In Philippians one, the apostle tells those dear saints that he is sure that God who has begun the good work in them, will perform it until the day of Jesus Christ. In verses nine to eleven of this chapter, he says, "And this I pray, that your love may abound yet more and more in knowledge and in all judgment; that ye may approve things that are excellent; that ye may be sincere and without offence till the day of Christ; being filled with the fruits of righteousness, which are by Jesus Christ, unto the glory and praise of God." It seems to me that every one ought to understand that a life that is lived for God is one bringing forth the fruits of righteousness. Love, purity, goodness, sweetness, kindness, compassion, consideration for others, all of these things are the beautiful fruits that grow in this garden when the living water is properly fructifying the soil. In Galatians 5 : 22 we have a long list of the fruit of the Spirit. Challenge your own heart by asking, "Am I producing this kind of fruit for Him, 'Love, joy, peace, longsuffering' ?" It is that patience, you know, that makes you willing to endure. Then there is "gentleness, goodness, faith, meekness, temperance." This is the delightful fruit that our Lord is looking for in the lives of His people. He would have every one of us as a garden that produces fruit like this.

That word translated "orchard" is really similar to the Persian word for "Paradise," and it may suggest that as God has a paradise above for His own people, where they shall share His joy for all eternity, so a believer's heart when it is producing fruit like this, is for God a paradise where He finds His joy and His delight. I wonder if we think enough

of that side of it. Are we not likely to become
self-centered and merely think of God as serving us, the blessed Lord Jesus giving Himself
for us, dying for us, rising again for us, nur-
turing our souls, guiding us through the wil-
derness of this world and bringing us at last to
glory? Some of the hymns we sing are almost
entirely occupied with the blessings that come
to us, but these do not rise to the height of the
Christian's communion at all. It is when we
are through thinking about what God is doing
for us, and are seeking by grace to adore the
One who does all this for us, and are letting
our lives go out to Him as a thank-offering
in praise and adoration, that we truly rise to
the height of our Christian privileges. Then
it is that He gathers these sweet and lovely
fruits in His garden. It is not only fruit upon
which He feeds, but it is that which gives satisfaction in every sense. "Camphire, with spikenard, spikenard and saffron; calamus and cinnamon, with all trees of frankincense; myrrh
and aloes, with all the chief spices." Some
of these plants give forth their fragrance as
the rain and dew fall upon them; some of
them send forth a subtle aroma when the rays

of the sun are warming them. Others never exude, never give out their fragrance, until they are pierced and the sap flows forth. So is it with our lives. We need all kinds of varied experiences in order that we may manifest the graces of Christ in our behavior, and it is not only that we are to be for His delight in the sense in which I have been speaking, but we are to be for His service too, in making known His grace to a lost world.

In the next verse we read, "A fountain of gardens, a well of living waters, and streams from Lebanon." Let us see if we can correlate that. There is Lebanon, that backbone mountain range of Palestine, with Mt. Hermon to the north covered with snow. The streams coming down from Lebanon sink into the ground, and as they do so, springs rise here and there in vales and dells to the surface of the earth, and so the living water flows forth to refresh the thirsty soil. The living water represents, as we know from John's Gospel, the blessed Holy Spirit. Our Lord Jesus said, "If any man thirst, let him come unto Me and drink. He that believeth on Me, as the Scripture hath said, from within

him shall flow rivers of living water. But this
spake He of the Spirit, which they that believe
on Him should receive: for the Holy Ghost was
not yet given; because that Jesus was not yet
glorified" (John 7 : 37-39).

Now the Spirit of God descending from
above enters into our inmost being and then we
have the living water springing up unto everlasting life. Our own hearts are refreshed and
gladdened, and the living water in abundance
flows out from us for the blessing of a lost
world around. Is this not a beautiful picture?
My brother, my sister, what do you know of
this life in the fulness of the Holy Spirit? Far
too many of us seem to be content to know
that our sins have been forgiven, that we have
a hope of heaven based upon some testimony
that we have received from Holy Scripture.
But it is more than this. We are not merely
to have the assurance of our own salvation,
but every one of us should be as watered
gardens for Him, with streams flowing out for
the refreshment of dying men and women all
about us.

In what measure is your life touching others?
In what measure are you being used of God

to win other souls for Christ? If we have to confess, as many of us would, that we have never had the privilege of winning one soul, that so far as we know we have never yet given a testimony to any one that has really been blessed in his or her coming to Christ, let me suggest that there must be something that is hindering the outflow of the living water. Can it be that great boulders of worldliness, selfishness, pride, carnality, sinful folly or covetousness are literally choking the fountain of living water, so that there is just a little trickling when there should be a wonderful outflowing? If this is the case, seek by grace to recognize these hindrances and deal with them one by one. Away with worldliness, away with pride. Who am I to be proud? What have I to be proud of? "What hast thou that thou hast not received?" Away with carnality, away with self-seeking, away with covetousness, away with living for my own interests, and let me henceforth live alone for Him who shed His precious blood for me and redeemed me to Himself. As I thus deal with these things that hinder the outflow of the living water, I will myself enter into a new, living, blessed and wonderful experience, and my testimony then will count in blessing to those about me, and my life will be at its best for Him.

There has been some question as to the identity of the first speaker in verse sixteen. It is very evident that the one who speaks in the last sentence is the bride, but is it the bride or the bridegroom in the first part of the verse? "Awake, O north wind; and come, thou south; blow upon my garden, that the spices thereof may flow out." If it is the bridegroom who is speaking, then he it is who is calling on the winds to blow upon what he calls, "my garden," the heart of his bride, in order that she may be at her best for him. If, on the other hand, as I am personally inclined to believe, it is the bride who is speaking, then it indicates her yearning desire to be all that he would have her to be. Dear child of God, is that your desire? Do you yearn to be all that Christ would have you to be, or are you still actuated by worldly and selfish motives that hinder communion with Him? Listen to these words again, as we think of them as coming from the lips of the bride, "Awake, O north wind." That is the cold, bitter, biting, wintry blast. Naturally she would shrink from that as we all would, and yet the cold of winter is as necessary as the warmth of summer if there is going to be perfection in fruit-bearing. It is as though she says, "Blessed God, if need be, let Thy Spirit breathe upon me through trial and sorrow, and difficulty and perplexity; take from me all in which I have trusted from the human standpoint; bereave me of everything if Thou wilt; leave me cold, naked, and alone except for Thy love, but work out Thy will in me."

The best apples are grown in northern climes where frost and cold have to be faced. Those grown in semi-tropical countries are apt to be tasteless and insipid. It takes the cold to bring out the flavor. And it is so with our lives. We need the north winds of adversity and trial as well as the zephyrs of the south so agreeable to our natures. The very things we shrink from are the experiences that will work in us to produce the peaceable fruits of righteousness. If everything were easy and soft and beautiful in our lives, they would be insipid; there would be so little in them for God that could delight His heart; and so there must be the north wind as well as the south. But, on the other hand, we need the south wind also, and our precious Lord tempers the winds to every one of us. "Awake, O north wind; and come, thou south; blow upon my garden, that the spices thereof may flow out." It is a blessed thing to be in that state of soul where we can just trust ourselves to Him.

Charles Spurgeon tells of a man who had the words, "God is love," painted on his weathervane. Some one said, "That is a queer text to put there. Do you mean to say that God's love is as changeable as the wind?" "Oh, no," said the other; "I mean that whichever way the wind blows, God is love." Do not forget that. It may be the north wind of bereavement when your dearest and best are snatched from you, but "God is love." It may be that the cold wind of what the world calls ill-fortune will sweep away like a fearful cyclone all that you have accumulated for years, but "God is love," and it is written, "The Lord hath His way in the whirlwind and in the storm, and the clouds are the dust of His feet" (Nah. 1: 3).

Perhaps you have been asking questions like this, "Why has God allowed the sufferings we have had to undergo? Why has He allowed these weeks and months with no employment and everything slipping away, the savings of years gone?" Dear child of God, He giveth not account of any of His matters now, but,

> "When you stand with Christ in glory,
> Looking o'er life's finished story,"

then He will make it clear to you, and you will know why He allowed the cold wind to blow over His garden as well as the south wind, and if you would bow to Him now, and recognize His unchanging love, perhaps He would be able to trust you with more zephyrs from the south than you ordinarily experience. We are not subject enough to the will of God. We need to learn the lesson that, "All things work together for good to them that love God, to them who are the called according to His purpose" (Rom. 8:28).

"Awake, O north wind; and come, thou south; blow upon my garden, that the spices thereof may flow out." In other words, "Anything, Lord, that will make me a better Christian, a more devoted saint; anything that will make me a more faithful child of Thine, so that Thou canst find Thy delight in me." Is that your thought? And then she looks up into the face of her bridegroom and says, "Let my beloved come into his garden, and eat his pleasant fruits." How He delights to get such an invitation as that from His people. He responds to her immediately, for the first verse of chapter five really belongs to this section. She no sooner says, "Come," than he replies, "I am come into my garden, my sister, my spouse: I have gathered my myrrh with my spice; I have eaten my honeycomb with my honey; I have drunk my wine with my milk: eat, O friends; drink, yea, drink abundantly, O beloved."

It closes with a scene of rapturous communion. And when you look up to the Beloved of your heart and say, "Come into Thy garden and eat Thy pleasant fruits," He will immediately respond, "I am come." You will never have to wait; you will never have to give Him a second invitation. If you have any time for Him, He always has time for you.

VI

"I sleep, but my heart waketh; it is the voice of my beloved that knocketh, saying, Open to me, my sister, my love, my dove, my undefiled: for my head is filled with dew, and my locks with the drops of the night. I have put off my coat; how shall I put it on? I have washed my feet; how shall I defile them? My beloved put in his hand by the hole of the door, and my bowels were moved for him. I rose up to open to my beloved; and my hands dropped with myrrh, and my fingers with sweet smelling myrrh, upon the handles of the lock. I opened to my beloved; but my beloved had withdrawn himself, and was gone: my soul failed when he spake: I sought him, but I could not find him; I called him, but he gave me no answer. The watchmen that went about the city found me, they smote me, they wounded me; the keepers of the walls took away my veil from me. I charge you, O daughters of Jerusalem, if ye find my beloved, that ye tell him, that I am sick of love" (Song of Solomon 5: 2-8).

WE have a very long section before us beginning with the second verse of chapter five and concluding with the fifth verse of chapter eight. In this entire portion we have traced out for us in a very wonderful way the interruption of communion and its final restoration. We have already had one similar picture in this book where the bridegroom's absence produced a temporary sense of estrangement. We have that dealt with more fully in this section, where the bridegroom's advances are coldly spurned. If we will remember that the bride speaks of any regenerated soul and that the bridegroom is our blessed Lord Jesus Christ, I am sure we shall have no difficulty in getting the spiritual lesson of these chapters.

We have all experienced interrupted communion. We have all known such periods of glad joy in the Lord as those brought before us in the previous chapter. But how often have we found that, following almost immediately on a period of great blessing and delightful fellowship with the Lord, there may come a time of spiritual dearth and broken fellowship. You recall that in Israel's history they were scarcely through rejoicing over the wonderful victory at Jericho before they were wringing their hands in despair because of the defeat at Ai. How often in our Christian lives we have similar experiences. Perhaps you go to an edifying meeting where your whole soul is stirred by the singing, by the prayers, and by the ministry of the Word, and you feel as though you would never again lose sight of your blessed Redeemer's face; and yet the spirit is willing but the flesh is weak, and within a very short time you find yourself inquiring,

> "Where is the blessedness I knew
> When first I saw the Lord?"

And everything seems dark and cloudy and you no longer discern your Saviour's presence. Is there any one who has had uninterrupted communion with the Lord throughout all the years? I am sure there is not. Even if we imagined so, it would simply be because we lacked that sensitiveness which would enable us to apprehend the fact that He was in some sense grieved because of our behavior.

We have a wonderfully beautiful picture here. The bride has retired and she is drowsing, just about asleep, and yet a bit restless, when there comes a knock at the door. It is the knock of the beloved one who has returned from a distant journey and he cries, "Open to me, my sister, my love, my dove, my undefiled;

for my head is filled with dew, and my locks with the drops of the night." We have the same picture in the New Testament in the third chapter of the book of Revelation, in which we see the Lord Jesus waiting outside the door of the Laodicean church. He says, "Behold, I stand at the door and knock: if any man hear My voice, and open the door, I will come in to him, and will sup with him, and he with Me." But what lethargy there is! How few respond to His gracious request! And so here the bride exclaims, "I have put off my coat; how shall I put it on? I have washed my feet; how shall I defile them?" There is a fretfulness about it. Why am I disturbed at this hour? Why did you not come at some other time? I have taken off my coat; why should I put it on now? I have washed my feet; why should I defile them? This refers to the eastern custom of washing the feet before seeking repose, for in that land they wore sandals and the upper part of the foot had no covering. In other words, she did not want to bestir herself even so much as to open the door to him. Have you never known similar experiences?

Have you never been so much concerned with your own affairs, with seeking your own ease, with self-pleasing, that when His voice called you for an hour of communion and fellowship with Him, you really repelled His advances, instead of gladly throwing open the door and saying, "Blessed Lord, nothing else is worthwhile but to enjoy the sunshine of Thy smile, to enjoy fellowship with Thyself?"

In this instance, we may see in the bride's behavior evidence of just such a state of soul. But then, as she lies there drowsing, neither actually asleep nor awake, she discerns something that moves her heart. She says, "My beloved put in his hand by the hole of the door." We will not understand the simile unless we are familiar with those eastern doors and locks. The lock was on the inside of the door, and there was an opening where the owner could, if he had the key, reach in and use the key from the inside to open the door. He comes, but he does not open the door in that way. He has asked admission and wants her to rise and open for him. She sees that hand come through the opening and the moment she does so, her heart is stirred and she

cries, "Oh, I must let him in." And now she
rises and hurries to the door and even as she
lays hold of the lock, she exclaims, "My hands
dropped with myrrh, and my fingers with
sweet-smelling myrrh, upon the handles of the
lock." That refers to another eastern custom.
When a lover came to visit the one who had
won his heart and found that she was not at
home, or if at home, she did not respond to
his advances, he covered the lock of the door
with sweet-smelling ointments and left flowers as a token of his affection. And so the
bride says, "My hands dropped with myrrh,
and my fingers with sweet-smelling myrrh."
It was not a dream then; he had really been
there and had gone. But she threw the door
open to enable him to hear her cry, "Come,
come in!" but there was no answering response.
"My beloved," she said, "had withdrawn himself and was gone."

Love is very sensitive. The trouble with
many of us is that we fail to recognize this.
We have an idea that the beloved one should
be ready whenever we are for a time of gladness together, but it is not always so. And so,
sometimes when He comes to the heart's door

we practically say, "No; it is inconvenient. I do not want to drop things right now." But later when we would enjoy His presence we find He has gone. Have you never had such experiences? Has He come to you and said, "I want you to sit down with Me over My Word; I want you to spend a little time in prayer; to dismiss other things from your mind and commune with Me," and you have said, "Oh, but I have so much to occupy me; I cannot do it now." Plenty of time for self but very little for Him. And then some wonderful token of His loving-kindness came to you, and you said, "Oh, I must respond to His heart," and you threw open the door as it were and called, but He was not there. And did you ever know what it was to go on for days and weeks without any real sense of His presence? "My beloved had withdrawn himself." If you do not respond to His voice when He comes to you in tender grace, you may seek Him for a long time before you will enjoy fellowship with Him again. Such is the sensitiveness of love. He wants to make you feel that His love is worthwhile, and wants to test you as to whether you are really in earnest when you profess to desire fellowship with Him.

And so as the story goes on, she leaves the house and goes out into the city seeking after him, and as she makes her way from street to street, perchance calling his name and looking here and there and wondering where he has hidden himself, she says, "The watchmen that went about the city found me, they smote me, they wounded me; the keepers of the walls took away my veil from me." You will always have to suffer if you refuse obedience to the voice of Christ when He calls you. You will always have to be tested before communion is restored.

There is a word in the New Testament that has troubled some of our sisters. In 1 Corinthians 11 we are told that a Christian woman, when she is engaged in worship with the people of God or in public prayer or testimony, is to cover her head with a veil. And people say, "Why the veil?" The Bible says that the veil is her "power." Is not that a strange thing? In the margin of our Bible we have a rather peculiar interpretation of that. I think it must have been suggested by a man. It says, "Power, a sign that she is under the power of her husband." But I do not think that is it, at all. This verse, I believe, explains what it means.

The covering on her head is her power. In what sense? Look at it this way. As long as her head was veiled that was her power, but when the keepers saw her going about the streets at night, they misunderstood her motive and character, and they took away her veil. The unveiled woman was marked out as one who was unclean and unchaste; but the covering on her head was the sign of the chaste and modest wife or maiden.

Years ago I was a Salvation Army officer. I remember that our Army girls could go anywhere with those little blue bonnets. I never knew but one in all the years I was connected with them, who was insulted by any one in any place as long as she had that little bonnet on. I have been seeking the lost in the lowest kind of dives on the Barbary Coast of San Francisco, and have seen them come in with their papers and go from one rough ungodly man to another, and ordinarily no one ever said an unkind or a wicked word to them. But once a drunken sailor dared to say something insulting to one of them, immediately practically the entire crowd jumped on him and knocked him down and gave him such a trouncing as

he had never had before; and then threw him
into the street for the police to pick up. The
little blue bonnet was the power of the Salvation Army lassie. Just so the covered head
of the women in that oriental land. The un-
covered head bespoke the immoral woman,
while the covered head was her power, and
told that she was seeking to live a life of
goodness and purity. So here, because the
bride has lost the sense of her bridegroom's
presence, she is branded as though she were
impure and unholy. This shame has come
upon her because she did not immediately respond to her bridegroom's call.

She turns for help to the daughters of Jerusalem as the morning dawns and she sees them
coming down the street. "I charge you, O
daughters of Jerusalem, if ye find my beloved,
that ye tell him, that I am sick of love." In
other words, Tell him my heart is yearning for
him; tell him I repent of my indifference, of
my cold-heartedness and my unconcern, and
want him above everything else. Christian, is
that what your heart says? Are you a backslidden believer? Do you remember times
when you enjoyed communion with your Lord,

when life with Him was sweet and precious indeed? But alas, alas, that fellowship has been broken, and you are saying with Job, "Oh, that I knew where I might find Him!" Does your heart say today, "Tell Him that I am sick of love, that my whole being is yearning after Him; I want to be restored to Him, to the sweetness of communion?" The daughters of Jerusalem say, "What is thy beloved more than another beloved, O thou fairest among women? What is thy beloved more than another beloved, that thou dost so charge us?"

This one that you say means so much to you, why is he more to you than you might expect another to be to us? The world says, "Why is Christ more to you than any other?" Why does Jesus mean so much more to us than the things that you and I have known in the world? "Tell us that we may seek him with thee." Then at once she begins to praise him and laud him. From verse ten to the end of the chapter in wonderful oriental imagery she praises his kindness, his graciousness, his aptness to help, his strength, and his tenderness. She cries, "My beloved is the chiefest among ten thousand." And when she thus praises him they turn again and say, "Where has he gone? How is it that you have let him slip out of your sight if he is so much to you?" Is that not a proper question? If Christ is so precious to you, if He means so much to you, why is it that you so easily allow fellowship to be broken? Why do you so readily permit other things to come in and hinder communion?

"Whither is thy beloved gone, O thou fairest among women? Whither is thy beloved turned aside? that we may seek him with thee." And then instantly as she bears testimony to him, she recalls the last words he said to her before that eventful night, "I am come into my garden," and her own heart was the garden, and she says, "I know where he is. My beloved is gone down into his garden, to the beds of spices, to feed in the gardens, and to gather lilies." And instantly he speaks; he is right there. He had been waiting and watching for her to come to the place where he was everything to her soul, and at once he exclaims, "Thou art beautiful, O my love, as Tirzah, comely as Jerusalem, terrible as an army with banners." And then through all the rest of the chapter he praises her; he expresses his appreciation of her as she had expressed hers of him. In chapter seven, verses one to nine, he uses one beautiful figure after another to tell all his delight in her. It is a wonderful thing to know that the Lord has far more delight in His people than we ourselves have ever had in Him. Some day we shall enjoy Him to the fullest; some day He will be everything to us; but as long as we are here, we never appreciate Him as much as He appreciates us. But as she listens to his expression of love, her heart is assured; she has the sense of restoration and fellowship. In verse ten she says, "I am my beloved's, and his desire is toward me." In other words, he has not turned against her. When we turn from Him, the natural thought of our hearts is that He has turned against us, but He has not. If He allows us to go through trial, it is like Joseph testing his brethren in order to see if there was genuine repentance of sin.

Three times in this little book we have similar expressions to this, "I am my beloved's and his desire is toward me." In chapter two, verse sixteen, we read, "My beloved is mine, and I am his." That is very precious. Are you

able to say, "My beloved is mine, and I am
His?" In other words, Have you given yourself to Him? Have you trusted Him as your
Saviour? If you have, He has given Himself
to you. Just the very moment you give yourself to Him in faith, that moment He gives
Himself to you and comes to dwell in your
heart. This is the assurance, then, of salvation. "My beloved is mine, and I am His."
And then in chapter six, verse three, she says,
"I am my beloved's, and my beloved is mine."
That is communion. I belong to him and he
belongs to me, that we may enjoy one another
together. And then in verse ten of chapter
seven, we read, "I am my beloved's, and his
desire is toward me." Every doubt and every
fear is gone. She has found her satisfaction
in him and he finds his in her. What a
wonderful picture! Shall it be only a picture, or is it to be a reality in our lives ?
Is it not a fact that so often we do the very
things the Shulamite did? So often we turn a
deaf ear to the Bridegroom's voice. We can
be so busy even with Christian work that we
do not take time for Him. I can be so occupied with preaching that I do not have time

for prayer. I can be so taken up with preparing sermons that I do not have time to feed on the Word. You may ask, "Why, how can you prepare sermons without feeding on the Word?" It is one thing to study the Bible in order to prepare an address which I am to give to other people, but it is another thing to sit down quietly in the presence of the Lord and say, "Blessed Saviour, as I open Thy Book I want to hear Thy voice speaking to my heart. I want Thee to talk to me, to express Thyself to me in tones of tender love." As I read in that attitude, He speaks to my soul, and as I lift my heart to Him in prayer, I talk with Him. That is communion.

Do not be content with the knowledge of salvation; do not be content to know that your soul is eternally secure; do not be content to know that you are serving Him in some little measure. Remember, there is something that means more to Him than all your service, and that is to sit at His feet and delight your soul in His love. As you read this description in the sixth chapter it will remind you of the fulness there is in Christ. It seems as though every figure is exhausted to show His wonder.

"Join all the glorious names
Of wisdom, love, and power,
That angels ever knew,
That mortals ever bore;
All are too mean to speak His worth,
Too mean to set the Saviour forth."

Oh, to have the heart so occupied with Him that we shall lose sight of everything else, and Christ alone will satisfy every longing of our souls!

VII

"Set me as a seal upon thine heart, as a seal upon thine arm: for love is strong as death; jealousy is cruel as the grave: the coals thereof are coals of fire, which hath a most vehement flame. Many waters cannot quench love, neither can the floods drown it: if a man would give all the substance of his house for love, it would utterly be contemned" (Song of Solomon 8: 6, 7).

IT is, of course, the love of the bridegroom for his bride that is thus spoken of. We have been tracing the manifestations of it throughout this little book, from the time when the shepherd first looked upon the shepherdess and his heart went out to her until the time when they were united in marriage. It is a beautiful picture, first of the love of Christ reaching us in our deep, deep need, and then that glorious union with Him which will be consummated at the marriage supper of the Lamb.

Now you hear the bride exclaiming, "Set me as a seal upon thine heart, as a seal upon thine

arm." The seal speaks of something that is
settled. One draws up a legal document and
seals it and that settles it. And so Christ and
His loved ones have entered into an eternal
relationship, and He has given us the seal, the
Holy Spirit. "Upon believing, ye were sealed
with that Holy Spirit of promise." This is
"the earnest of our inheritance until the redemption of the purchased possession." That
seal is the pledge of His love, and you will
notice that in the words that follow we have
love spoken of in four ways, at least we have
four characteristics of love.

First, there is the strength of love. "Love
is strong as death." Second, the jealousy of
love. In our Version we read, "Jealousy is
cruel as the grave," and of course that is often
true of human love. It may be a very cruel
thing indeed, but actually the word translated
"cruel" is the ordinary Hebrew word for "firm"
or "unyielding." It may be translated, "Jealousy is unyielding as the grave." "The coals
thereof are coals of fire, a vehement flame," and
this expression, "a vehement flame," in the
Hebrew text is "a flame of Jah." That is the
first part of the name of Jehovah and it is one

of the titles of God. In the third place we have
the endurance of love. "Many waters cannot
quench love, neither can the floods drown it."
And then lastly, the value of love. "If a man
would give all the substance of his house for
love, it would utterly be contemned."

First let us meditate on the strength of love;
and we are thinking, of course, of the love of
our God as revealed in the Lord Jesus Christ,
for Christ is the Bridegroom of our souls.
"Love is strong as death." This He has already demonstrated. "Christ loved the Church
and gave Himself for it." And that giving
Himself meant going into death to redeem His
own. "Love is strong as death." We might
even say in His case, "It is stronger than
death," for death could not quench His love.
He went down into death and came up in tri-
umph that He might make us His own, and it
is of this we are reminded as we gather at the
Lord's table. It is this which He wishes us to
cherish in a special way when we come together
to remember Him. He knows how apt we are
to forget; He knows how easy it is to be occupied with the ordinary things of life, and even
with the work of the Lord, and forget for the

moment the price He paid for our redemption;
and He would call us back from time to time to
sit together in sweetest and most solemn fellowship, and meditate on that mighty love of
His which is "strong as death." Nothing could
turn Him aside.

> "Love that no thought can reach,
> Love that no tongue can teach,
> Matchless it is!"

Because there was no other way to redeem
our souls, "He stedfastly set His face to go to
Jerusalem." When He went through that
Samaritan village, they did not receive Him
because they realized that there was no desire
upon His part to remain among them at that
time, but they saw "His face as though He
would go to Jerusalem," and they said as it
were, "Well, if He prefers to go to Jerusalem
rather than remain here with us, we are not
going to pay attention to His message. We are
not interested in the proclamation that He
brings." How little they understood that it
was for them, as truly as for the Jews in
yonder Judea, that He "set His face stedfastly
to go to Jerusalem." If He had not gone to
Jerusalem and given Himself up to the death

of the Cross, there could be no salvation for
Samaritan, Jew, or Gentile. But oh, the
strength of His love! He allowed nothing to
divert Him from that purpose for which He
had come from heaven. Before He left the
glory, He said, "Lo, I come (in the volume of
the book it is written of Me,) to do Thy will,
O God" (Heb. 10: 7). And to do the will of
God meant for Him laying down His life on the
cross for our redemption. Do we think of it
as much as we should? Do we give ourselves
to meditation, to dwelling on the love of
Christ, a love that passeth knowledge, and do
we often say to ourselves, "The Son of God
loved me, and gave Himself for me"? Oh, the
strength of His love!

Then we think of the jealousy of love. I
know that jealousy in these poor hearts of ours
is often a most contemptible and despicable thing. Jealousy on our part generally
means utter selfishness. We are so completely
selfish, we do not like to share our friends with
any one else; and what untold sorrow has come
into many a home because of the unreasonable
jealousy of a husband, of a wife, of parents,
or of children. But while we deprecate a

jealousy which has selfishness and sin at the
root of it, there is another jealousy which is
absolutely pure and holy, and even on our lower
plane some one has well said that, "Love is only
genuine as long as it is jealous." When the
husband reaches the place where he says, "I
do not care how my wife bestows her favors on
others; I do not care how much she runs around
with other men; I am so large-hearted I can
share her with everybody," that husband does
not love his wife, and if you could imagine a
wife talking like that about her husband, you
would know that love was gone, that it was
dead.

Love cannot but be jealous, but let us see that
it is a jealousy that is free from mere selfishness and unwarranted suspicion. When we
think of it in connection with God we remember that one of the first things we learned to
recite was the Ten Commandments, and some
of us were perplexed when we read, "I the
Lord thy God am a jealous God, visiting the
iniquity of the fathers upon the children unto
the third and fourth generation of them that
hate Me." We shrank back from that because
we were so used to thinking of jealousy as a

despicable human passion, that we could not think of God having it in His character. But it is He who has a right to be jealous. God's jealousy is as pure as is His love, and it is because He loves us so tenderly that He is jealous. In what sense is He jealous? Knowing that our souls' happiness and blessing alone will be found in walking in fellowship with Himself, He loves us so much He does not want to see us turning away from the enjoyment of His love and trying to find satisfaction in any lesser affection, which can only be for harm and eventual ruin. "The end of these things is death."

Paul writing to the Corinthian church says, "I am jealous over you with a godly jealousy, for I have espoused you to one husband, that I may present you a chaste virgin to Christ." And then he gives the ground of his jealousy. "But I fear, lest by any means, as the serpent beguiled Eve through his subtilty, so your minds should be corrupted from the simplicity that is in Christ." You see Paul was a true pastor. He loved the people of Christ's flock and knew that their only lasting joy was to be found in living in communion with their Saviour; and His heart was torn with a holy jealousy if he saw them turning aside to the things of the world, following after the things of the flesh, or being ensnared by the devil. Every God-anointed pastor will feel that way.

Young believers sometimes imagine that some of us who try to lead the flock of God are often needlessly hard and severe, and they think us unsympathetic and lacking in compassion and tenderness when we earnestly warn them of the folly of worldliness and carnality. They say, "Oh, they don't understand. That old fogy preacher, I have no doubt, had his fling when he was young, and now he is old and these things no longer interest him, and so he wants to keep us from having a good time!"

Let me "speak as a fool," and yet I trust to the glory of God. As a young believer coming to Christ when I was fourteen years old, the first lesson I had to learn was that there is nothing in this poor world to satisfy the heart, and by the grace of God I sought to give it all up for Jesus' sake. The only regret I have today is that there have ever been times in my life when I have drifted into carnality and fallen into a low backslidden state, and so allowed myself

something which afterward left a bad con-
science and a sense of broken fellowship, and
I never was happy until it was judged, and
I was once more in communion with the Lord.
If sometimes we speak strongly to you about
going in the ways of the world, reminding you
that God has said, "Come out from among
them, and be ye separate, and touch not the
unclean thing," it is because we have learned
by years of experience that there is no peace,
there is no lasting joy, there is no true un-
spoiled happiness for those who walk in the
ways of the world. If you want a life of gladness, a life of enduring bliss; if you want to
be able to lie down at last and face death with
a glad, free spirit, then we beg of you, follow
the path that your blessed Lord Jesus took. Oh
that we might not be turned aside but that we
might rouse our souls to a godly jealousy.

I wonder if you have ever noticed that the
blessed Holy Spirit who dwells in every believer is Himself spoken of as jealous. There
is a passage found in James 4: 4, 5, that I am
afraid is not often really understood, because
of the way it is translated in our Version, but
it is a very striking one: "Ye adulterers and

adulteresses, know ye not that the friendship of the world is enmity with God? Whosoever therefore will be a friend of the world is the enemy of God. Do ye think that the Scripture saith in vain, The Spirit that dwelleth in us lusteth to envy?" Take that home, dear young Christian. Do not be seduced by the world and its folly; do not be turned aside from the path of faithfulness to Christ by the mad rush for worldly pleasure and amusement; do not allow the flesh to turn you away and rob you of what should be your chief joy. "The friendship of the world is enmity with God. Whosoever therefore will be a friend of the world is the enemy of God.'" It is the next verse that perhaps we might not understand. "Do ye think that the Scripture saith in vain, The Spirit that dwelleth in us lusteth to envy?" One might gather that this expression, "The Spirit that dwelleth in us lusteth to envy," was a quotation from Scripture, as though He were asking, "Do you think the Scripture, that is, the Old Testament, saith in vain, 'The Spirit that dwelleth in us lusteth to envy?' " But you can search the Old Testament from the beginning of Genesis to the end of Malachi, and you will not find those words or anything that sounds like them. So it is clear that that is not what is meant. In fact, there are really two distinct questions in the Greek. First there is the question, "Do ye think that the Scripture speaketh in vain?" Do you? Do you think that the Scripture speaks in vain? Having read its warnings and its admonitions against worldliness, against the unequal yoke, against the pleasures of sin, against following the path of the flesh, do you sometimes say in your heart, "I know it is all in the Bible, but after all, I am not going to take it too seriously?" Do you think that the Scripture speaketh in vain?

Why has God put these things in His Word? Is it because He does not love you, and desires to keep you from things that would do you good? That is what the devil told Eve in the beginning. He insinuated that God did not love her. He said, "God doth know that in the day ye eat thereof, then your eyes shall be opened, and ye shall be as gods, knowing good and evil" (Gen. 3:5). And Eve said, "I am going to eat of it; I will try anything once." Is that what you have been saying too? If you

can only do this or do that, you think you will
have an experience you have never had before.
The whole world is looking for new thrills today. Before you act, put the question to yourself, "Does the Scripture speak in vain?" It
tells you that the end of all these things is
death and you may be assured the Scripture
does *not* speak in vain.

Then there is a second question, "Doth the
Spirit that dwelleth in us jealously desire?"
And the answer is, "Yes." The Holy Ghost
dwelling in the believer jealously desires to
keep us away from the world and to keep our
hearts true to Christ. Do you realize that you
never tried to go into anything that dishonored
the Lord, you never took a step to go into the
world, but the Spirit of God within you was
grieved, and sought to exercise you because He
jealously desired to keep you faithful to Christ?
I am talking to Christians. If you are not a
Christian, the Spirit does not dwell in you, and
you do not know what this is.

Our blessed Lord wants you all for Himself.
People say sometimes, "Well, I want to give
the Lord the first place in my heart," and they
mean that there will be a lot of places for other

things. The Lord does not merely want the first place; He wants the whole place; He wants to control your whole heart, and when He has the entire control, everything you do will be done for His glory.

A striking little incident is told by Pastor Dolman. Before the world war he was in Russia holding some meetings in the palace of one of the Russian nobility. Among those who attended the meetings was a Grand Duchess. She was a sincere evangelical Christian. Dr. Dolman was talking one day about a life devoted to Christ, about separation and unworldliness, and when he finished, the Grand Duchess stepped forward and said, "I do not agree with everything Pastor Dolman said."

"What did I say with which you do not agree, Your Imperial Highness?" asked Dr. Dolman.

"You said it is wrong to go to the theater. I go to the theater, but I never go without first getting down on my knees and asking Him to go with me, and He does."

Pastor Dolman said, "But, Your Imperial Highness, I did not say a word about the theater."

"I know; but you meant that."

"Your Imperial Highness," said Dr. Dolman, "are you not turning things around? Who gave you or me authority to decide where we will go or what we will do, and then to ask the Lord to be with us in it? Instead of getting down on your knees and saying, 'Lord, I am going to the theater, come with me,' why don't you wait until He comes to you and says, 'Grand Duchess, I am going to the theater, and I want you to go with Me?' "

She threw up her hands and was honest enough to say, "Pastor Dolman, you have spoiled the theater for me. I cannot go again."

"Where He leads me, I will follow," but don't you start and ask Him to tag along. Let Him lead. Because He knows that your real, lasting happiness and joy are bound up in devotion to Him, He is jealous lest you should be turned aside.

Now we notice the endurance of love. "Many waters cannot quench love, neither can the floods drown it." How precious that is! How blessedly it was proven in His case. He went down beneath the floods of divine judgment. He could say, "Deep calleth unto deep at the

noise of Thy waterspouts: all Thy waves and
Thy billows are gone over Me" (Ps. 42:7).
But it did not quench His love, and through
all the years since His people have had to endure many things; they have had to pass
through deep waters, to go through great trials,
but He has been with them through it all. "In
all their affliction He was afflicted, and the
angel of His presence saved them" (Isa. 63:9).
In Isaiah 43:2 we read, "When thou passest
through the waters, I will be with thee; and
through the rivers, they shall not overflow
thee: when thou walkest through the fire, thou
shalt not be burned; neither shall the flame
kindle upon thee." Don't you love to have
somebody to whom you can go with all your
troubles and know He will never get tired of
you?

Some years ago I became acquainted with
a poor little old lady in a place where I was
ministering the Word. She was going through
all kinds of sorrow, and she came to me and
said, "I would just like to tell you about my
troubles." I felt like saying, "Dear sister, I
wish you would tell them to the Lord." But
I sat down and listened, and now for over ten

years I have been getting her troubles by mail,
and I try to send her a little encouraging and
sympathetic word in reply. Recently I met
her again and she said, "You must be getting
awfully tired of my troubles," and if I had
told the truth, I would have had to say, "Yes,
I am," but I said, "What is troubling you now?"
"Oh," she said, "it is not anything new, but it
is such a comfort to find somebody who will
enter into them and understand!" And she
was so effusive in her gratitude I was ashamed
that I had not entered into things more deeply.

Ah, we have a great High Priest who never
wearies of our trials. We weary of hearing
of them sometimes because they stir our hearts
and we would like to do that which we cannot
do; but He has power to see us through. No
trial, no distress, can quench His love. "Having loved His own which were in the world, He
loved them unto the end" (John 13:1). Somebody has translated it this way, "Having loved
His own which were in the world, He loved
them all the way through." Through what?
Through everything. He even loved Peter
through his denial, through his cursing and
swearing, and loved him back into fellowship

with Himself. His love is unfailing. Having taken us up in grace, He loves to the end.

Let us look now at the value of love. Can you purchase love? Can you pay for it? I was in a home at one time where a very rich man of seventy years of age, worth millions, had married a girl of eighteen. Her ambitious, worldly-minded mother had engineered the marriage. I could not help noticing that young wife off in a corner sobbing to herself and crying bitterly, but I tried never to interfere, for I did not want her to tell me what was in her heart. But one day the husband said, "Do you notice how downhearted my wife is?" I said, "She must have had some great sorrow."

"I am her sorrow," he said. "She was a poor girl, very beautiful and talented, and, as you know, I have been very successful, and I just thought that I could give her every comfort and could surely make her love me. I know that we do not seem to be suited; she is so much younger than I. But she can have everything, all the beautiful clothes and jewels she wants, and surely any girl ought to be happy in a home like this. But, you know, it is all in vain; I cannot seem to buy her love."

Of course not.   He ought to have known that
he did not have that in his heart to which she
could respond.   They belonged to two different
ages, as it were.   "Many waters cannot quench
love, neither can the floods drown it: if a man
would give all the substance of his house for
love, it would utterly be contemned."   You
cannot buy love, but oh, His love to us creates
love in us.   It is not the wonderful things that
He has done for us, it is not the fact that He
has enriched us for eternity, but it is because
of what He is.   "We love Him because He first
loved us."

> "His is an unchanging love,
>   Higher than the heights above;
>   Deeper than the depths beneath,
>   Free and faithful, strong as death."

What a blessed thing to know Him and love
Him and be loved by Him!   Oh, to be kept
from wounding such a Lover, from grieving
His Holy Spirit!   For we read, "The love of
God is shed abroad in our hearts by the Holy
Spirit which is given unto us."

VIII

"What shall we do for our sister?" (Song of Solomon 8:8).

THIS question was put by the bride to the bridegroom after she had been brought into the full enjoyment of the privileges that he delighted to lavish upon her. He had found her a shepherdess there in the hill country, and loved her and won her heart in those trying days when she felt herself so despised and neglected. Brought to the palace and united in marriage to the king, enjoying to the full his tender consideration and surrounded by the evidences of his affection, she could not keep from thinking of the little mountain home from which she had come.

She thought of the dear old mother who had raised her and cared for her after the father's death, for it is evident that the mother was a widow, and the family by superintending the king's vineyard earned a precarious living; and then she thought of the little sister, much younger than she, who had none of the privileges that she was enjoying. And as she thought of her, she seemed to say, "This bridegroom of mine, my king, the one who has loved me and brought me into these privileges, cannot but take an interest in my family, in my household, and I am going to speak to him about that sister of mine." And so she turned to him in the tenderest, most confiding way, and said, "I have a little sister, a little undeveloped sister, up there in the vineyard. I am concerned about her. Is there not something we could do for her? What shall we do for our sister?" And he responds at once, "If she be a wall, we will build upon her a palace of silver: and if she be a door, we will inclose her with boards of cedar." You see, this is just the oriental way of saying, "I am so glad you spoke to me about that little sister of yours; I am so glad that you have not forgotten her and her needs. It will be a real privilege for me to show my love for you by what I do for her." And so he uses the striking figures of the wall and the door as he asserts his willingness to help. It was as though he said, "Whatever her circumstances are, and whatever her needs

are, I will be delighted to minister to them and
I will make you my agent in doing it."

It seems to me this expresses one of the very
first evidences of union with Christ. We are
no sooner saved ourselves, no sooner rejoicing
in the knowledge of Christ as our Redeemer,
as the Lover of our souls, as our heavenly
Bridegroom, than we begin to think of others
less privileged, and our hearts cry out with
longing, "What about my little sister? What
about my brother? What about those who are
still in their sins and still in their deep deep
need, who do not know, do not understand this
incomprehensible love of Thine which means so
much to me?" And it is the Holy Spirit Himself who puts that yearning into our hearts that
leads us to manifest an interest in the souls
of others. In other words, every real Christian feels within him something that impels
him to missionary service.

Are you saved yourself? Then have you been
to the Lord about that little sister, or about
that neglected brother? Perhaps it is a little
sister or a brother you have never seen, and
maybe, strange to say, of an altogether different color from yours! Perhaps that little sister

of yours is away yonder, a child-widow in India, perhaps a down-trodden native woman in Central Africa, or a degraded Indian in the wilds of South America, but yet your little sister; for we read, "God hath made of one blood all nations that be upon the face of the earth." And while you may say, "But she is so sinful, so undeserving," you must remember that you too were sinful and undeserving and the grace that is lavished upon you came from His heart of love. He delights to give to the undeserving, and the very need of that little sister of yours is the reason why you should be going to the Lord about her.

The bride here is really praying about her sister. Do you often go to the blessed Lord in prayer for that little sister of yours? Perhaps it is a brother. My brother, you who rejoice in Christ Jesus, do you think very often of that poor, ignorant, under-privileged, degraded, sinful brother of yours, living perhaps in heathen darkness today, or dwelling in the slums of one of our great cities, or, it may be, enjoying all that this life has to offer and yet not knowing Christ? Have you been to Him about that degraded one? Somebody has said,

"A selfish Christian is a contradiction in terms," and yet we do hear people talking about selfish Christians. Christianity is the manifestation in the life of the love of Christ, and that same love which was lavished upon you He would now have you lavish upon others in their need. What wonderful pictures we have along this line!

In the beginning of John's Gospel we read how the Lord revealed Himself to one and another, and every one who got that divine revelation went after some one else. Each said, "I have a brother, a friend, a dear one in need, and I must go to that one and tell the story of Jesus; tell him that we have found Him." The privileges, the blessings that God has given to us in Christ are not given to us for ourselves alone. We may say in connection with them all: You must either use them or lose them. "What," you say, "are you telling us that we may lose our souls after having been truly converted?" That is not a blessing. Your soul is you. Of course you cannot lose that if it is saved. I recognize the fact that having life eternal, you shall never perish, but I am talking about the blessings that the Lord lavishes

upon you from day to day. They are in order
that you may share them with others. To what
extent do you enter into that?

I would have you think of three things. First,
to what extent do you use your time for the
blessing of other people? When I find Christians who need so much physical recreation and
have so little time to seek to win souls, I do not
quite understand it. I was speaking with a
young man some months ago, and I said, "Do
you do anything to win others for Christ?" He
said, "I would like to, but it doesn't seem to
be my gift. I work hard all day, and when
Saturday comes I have to go off and get some
physical exercise." I think his great invigorat-
ing exercise was throwing horse-shoes at a
little stick. I said, "Did it ever strike you that
you could get wonderful exercise by taking a
bundle of tracts and going out on a country road
and visiting the homes along the way, telling
people about their souls? Walking is wonderful exercise."

"But," he said, "you see, I am thinking of
serious things all week, and I cannot be serious
on Saturday afternoon." Time is given us to
use in view of eternity. I quite recognize that

we need a certain amount of physical exercise or we would go to pieces, but you will find you can get on beautifully if you give more of your time to God. I was saved forty-one years ago, and I can honestly say my best times ever since have been those in which I have spent my days trying to help other people to a knowl, edge of Christ, and it is the greatest exercise in the world. I was visiting a preacher some time ago, and he asked, "What do you do for physical exercise?" I replied, "I preach." "But I mean when you want to get a rest," he said. "I preach some more and that rests me," I answered; "the more you do in the work of the Lord, the better you feel." "Brother," he said, "you will have a nervous breakdown if you are not careful." "But I am trying to be careful," I said. It isn't the Lord's work that gives people nervous breakdowns, it is getting into debt, getting mixed up in questionable things, and then you get worried and upset. Just keep at solid service for the Lord Jesus Christ, and you will not have a nervous breakdown. Paul was at it for thirty years. They tried to kill him again and again; he was half-drowned several times, and was thrown to wild beasts, but the old man, when about seventy years of age, had much more vigor than a lot of worldly preachers that I meet, who have to go on a prolonged vacation every once in a while. Your time belongs to the Lord Jesus, and He gives it to you in order that you may use it to bless and help other folk. "Look not every man on his own things, but every man also on the things of others" (Phil. 2:4).

Some time ago, I knew a dear man, one of the greatest men for physical exercise I ever saw. He worked hard on the street railroad. I would see him down on his knees, a great big covering over his eyes to shield them from the brilliant light, as he welded the steel rails. By Saturday noon, he was just worn out, and he would get a bundle of books and off he would go for exercise, over the hills and far away, hunting up poor needy souls, maybe in the County Hospital, possibly in the jails, and to poor families. Sometimes he would hear of somebody lying sick and poor and miserable, and he would go to see that one. And you know he had a remarkable way of preaching the Gospel. He would often lay down a five-dollar bill at the side of the bed, if he found out that they had no money to pay the bills. On Sunday he would say, "My! I was worn out yesterday, but I had a wonderful time Saturday afternoon, and I am all rested up." He was living for others.

> "Live for others while on earth you live,
> Give for others what you have to give,"

and then you will find the secret of a really happy Christian life. Your time is to be spent in the service of Christ for the blessing of others, for the blessing of the little sister, of that poor brother.

And then there is something else. He has entrusted you with your talents. "Oh, but," you say, "I haven't any." Oh, yes; you have. You would not like it if others said you had none. But who are you using them for? For Christ, for the blessing of that brother, of that sister in need? It is the investment that you make of your talents here for the glory of the Lord Jesus Christ that is going to bring you a reward at His judgment-seat. You remember what He said, "Unto every one that hath shall be given...but from him that hath not shall be taken away even that which he hath."

You are to use the talents God has given you
for Jesus' sake. Is it the ability to speak?
Use it for winning souls to Christ. Is it that
you know how to be a kindly sympathetic
friend? Then surely you have a wonderful
sphere for service. Is it looking up the shut-
ins, the sick and needy, and giving them a tender loving word? You would bless and help so
many you never think of now, if you would only
begin to use those talents for Him. It is not
all the work of the man on the platform. I
never see souls coming to Christ in a meeting
but I wonder what started them. Years ago,
when I was young and ignorant, I would go
home to my wife and say, "I won six souls
tonight," and she would look at me and say,
"Are you sure *you* did it?" I would say, "No,"
of course, "but the Lord used me." But you
know it really began away back of that. Perhaps it was a dear Sunday School teacher who
had been sowing the seed in the heart of that
young man or woman. It was lying there
dormant for days, months, or years, and as the
Word of God came anew, something was said
that just caused it to fructify and burst into
life, and that boy or girl came to Jesus.

Perhaps it was the lesson the mother taught as the child knelt at her knee long ago. Perhaps it was the father's word dropped into the heart. There is seldom a soul who comes to Christ but there were a lot of folk who had to do with it. It is not just the preacher and the preached message. God give us to use our talents for Christ. Paul planted, Apollos watered, "but God gave the increase."

Then there is my privilege not only to use my time and my talents but my money, to help and bless that little sister, that neglected brother. What a wonderful thing consecrated money is! There never would have been a dollar bill, a piece of silver money, a gold, copper or nickel coin in the world, if it had not been for sin. That is why Jesus calls it the mammon of unrighteousness. Every coin in your pocket is a witness that sin has come into the world. If men and women had remained as they were when God created them, there would have been no money. People would not have sought to build up fortunes, and buy and sell things. We would still be living in a glorious state on this earth, and we would not have had to go out and earn our bread by the sweat of

our brow. And now Jesus says, "Make to your-
selves friends of the mammon of unrighteousness; that when ye fail, they may receive you
into everlasting habitations" (Luke 16 : 9).
Since the money is here, and we cannot get
along without it, do not live for it; do not let
it get a hold on you ("The love of money is
the root of all evil"), but use it now in refer-
ence to the everlasting habitations; use it to
meet, of course, your own needs and those of
your family, but then use it as God enables
you, to bless and help others in their deep
spiritual need and in their temporal need too.
Then, by-and-by, when at last you reach the
glorious habitation, you will see a throng running down the golden street to meet you, and
they will say, "Welcome," and you will ask in
amazement, "Who can these be?" And one
will answer, "We are so glad to welcome you
here, for it was your dollar that paid for that
Testament that brought me the message of
Christ." Another, "You met my need when in
such distress I thought nobody cared for me,
and then you gave me the money for a good
dinner, and I could not help but think of the
God of all grace who had put it in your heart

to do that for me"; and another, "I came to
Jesus because of the kind deed you did for me."
Then we will feel it was worthwhile that we
spent and were spent for others. "What shall
be done for our little sister?" Let us share
with her the good things we have.

The king says, "If she be a wall, we will
build upon her a palace of silver." A wall
speaks of security. If she has already entered
into the blessings of Christ, we will build upon
her a silver palace. We will add to that which
is already hers. We will try to help and lead
her on and build her up in the things which be
in Christ. "If she be a door, we will inclose
her with boards of cedar." A door speaks of
responsibility, or opportunity for service. "A
great door," says the apostle, "and effectual is
opened unto me, and there are many adver-
saries" (1 Cor. 16:9). "Behold, I have set before thee an open door, and no man can shut
it: for thou hast a little strength, and hast
kept My word, and hast not denied My name"
(Rev. 3:8). But what use is a door if it has
no side-posts to swing from? "If she be a
door, we will inclose her with boards of cedar."
If she wants an opportunity for service, we

will help to make it possible, and we will assist her in whatever is required, that she may work the better for the Lord Jesus Christ.

Then as the chapter closes and the little book closes, the bride, her heart content to think she has come into blessing and that her little sister too has come into blessing, goes over the past, and talks about the vineyard days, the love that has been shown and the bliss now hers, and then she turns to her beloved one and says, "Make haste, my beloved, and be thou like to a roe or to a young hart upon the mountains of spices." "Till the day break and the shadows flee away." The consummation of all bliss will be when we are at home forever with Him. Till then, let us seek to spend and be spent for His glory.

You have heard of the missionary offering that was being taken, and as the box was handed to a very wealthy man, he brushed it to one side and said, "I do not believe in missions." "Then," said the usher, "take something out; this is for the heathen." How can you be a real Christian and not be concerned about those who are less privileged than you are? God stir our hearts to think of the mil-

lions still in their great, great need.   If we can
do nothing else for them, we can bring their
case to Him; we can be prayer-helpers; we can
intercede on their behalf. The wonderful thing
is that when you begin to pray, the rest follows.
Men who pray devise ways and means for giving.   A lady said to me one time, "You know
my husband is unsaved, and he never lets me
have any money.   He says he wouldn't for the
world give me a dime to put in the missionary
offering.   But I started praying about missions, and as I prayed, there came such a
burden on my heart to do something.   I had
two or three chickens that I had bought with
a little money I received from doing some sew-
ing for a neighbor.   It was all mine, and I said,
'I am going to devote one chicken to the Lord,
and every egg that this chicken lays will belong
to Him.'   It has been wonderful to me to see
that the other chickens lay every once in a
while, but my husband growls and says, 'That
missionary chicken of yours lays nearly two
eggs a day.'   Of course that is an exaggeration,
but every little while I have another dozen
eggs, and I take them to the corner store and
get my money, and that goes for missions."   I

believe that the Lord will take that money and do with it what He did with the five loaves and two fishes: multiply, and multiply, and multiply them. Maybe one way in which He will multiply it will be to start some of you giving, and then, you see, the Lord will turn to this lady and say, "You are the woman that had that chicken the preacher told about. I am going to give you a part of the reward, for these folk just copied from you!"

Let us seek by grace to make every day count for the blessing of others. Loving Him truly we cannot be selfish or indifferent to the needs of those for whom He died, "until the day break and the shadows flee away."